PENGUIN BOOKS

THE PSYCHOLOGY OF STUPIDITY

Jean-François Marmion (editor) is a psychologist, an associate editor of the French journal *Sciences Humaines* [*Social Sciences*], and a former editor-in-chief of the French magazine *Le Cercle Psy* [*Psychological Circle*]. He lives in France, where *The Psychology of Stupidity* was a #1 bestseller.

the PSYCHOLOGY *of* STUPIDITY

Edited by Jean-François Marmion

Translated from the French by Liesl Schillinger

PENGUIN BOOKS

PENGUIN BOOKS
An imprint of Penguin Random House LLC
penguinrandomhouse.com

Originally published in French as *Psychologie de la connerie* by Sciences Humaines
Editions, Auxerre Cedex.

LIBRARY OF CONGRESS CATALOGING-IN-PUBLICATION DATA

Names: Marmion, Jean-François, editor.
Title: The psychology of stupidity / edited by Jean-François Marmion ;
translated from the French by Liesl Schillinger.
Description: New York : Penguin Books, 2020. | Includes bibliographical
references.
Identifiers: LCCN 2020006717 (print) | LCCN 2020006718 (ebook) |
ISBN 9780143134992 (trade paperback) | ISBN 9780525506652 (ebook)
Subjects: LCSH: Stupidity.
Classification: LCC BF431 .P8613 2020 (print) | LCC BF431 (ebook) |
DDC 155.7--dc23
LC record available at https://lccn.loc.gov/2020006717
LC ebook record available at https://lccn.loc.gov/2020006718

Printed in the United States of America
1   3   5   7   9   10   8   6   4   2

BOOK DESIGN BY LUCIA BERNARD

› CONTENTS ‹

ON STUPIDITY:
A WARNING

Abandon all hope, ye who enter here

"Good sense is the most equitably distributed thing in the world," wrote Descartes. And what about stupidity?

Whether it oozes or drips, trickles or gushes, it's everywhere. Without borders and without limits. Sometimes it emerges as a gentle, almost bearable lapping; other times as a nauseating, stagnant swamp. Still other times, it's an earthquake, a storm, or a tidal wave that engulfs everything in its path, smashing, trampling, befouling. No matter what form it takes, stupidity splatters us all. Rumor has it that we ourselves are the source of it. I am no exception.

The Unbearable Heaviness of Being

Everyone sees bullshit, listens to it, and reads it, every single day. At the same time, each of us is guilty of generating it, thinking it, mulling it, and speaking it aloud. We are all morons from time to time, spouting nonsense as we go about our lives, without any real consequences. The crucial thing is to be aware of it and to feel sorry about it; because to err is human, and admitting your faults is halfway to having them forgiven. There will always be those who take us for fools, but we recognize our own folly far too rarely. Apart from the perpetual purr of idiocy that surrounds us, day in, day out, there's also, sadly, the roar of the masters of stupidity, kings of stupidity—assholes with a capital *A*. Those assholes, whether you encounter them at work or at home, do not strike you as anecdotal. They hound you and harass you with their obstinacy in crass wrongheadedness, their unjustified arrogance. They prosper, they sign on the dotted line, and they would happily cross out all of your opinions, emotions, and dignity with one stroke of the pen. They erode your morale and make you doubt there can be any justice in this vile world. No matter how hard you try, you cannot detect a speck of kindred connection in them.

Stupidity is an unkept promise, a promise of intelligence and confidence that the idiots among us betray, traitors to humanity. These jerks are like dumb beasts—they're total animals! We might want to indulge them, to turn them into friends, but they're not on that level, which is to say, our level.

They suffer from a disease that has no cure. And since they refuse to heal themselves, convinced that they are one-eyed kings in the land of the blind, the tragicomedy is made complete. It's no surprise that people are fascinated by zombies—with the simulacrum of existence they embody, their intellectual vacuity, and their overwhelming, fundamental need to drag the living, the heroic, and the simply decent down to their own level. And that makes sense: idiots, like zombies, want to eat your brains: these failed human beings never fail you. The worst thing about them is that they can sometimes be intelligent, or at least make a show of it. They're so skilled at transforming the lineaments of learning to the bars of a cage that they would gladly burn books—along with their authors—in the name of some ideology, or of something they learned from some purported sage (idiotic or not).

Uncertainty Makes You Crazy, Certainty Makes You Stupid

Morons will condemn you instantly, with no appeal possible and no extenuating circumstances admitted, on the sole basis of the appearances they glimpse through their narrow blinkers. They know how to rouse their sympathizers, to goad them to lynching in the name of virtue, custom, respect. The idiot hunts in a pack and thinks in herd fashion. As the Georges Brassens song goes, "The plural is useless to mankind; whenever / More than four are gathered, you'll find a band of fools." He also declared: "Glory to the man who, lacking lofty ideals / Contents himself with not being a nuisance to his neighbors." Alas! Our neighbors don't always return the favor.

Not content with making you miserable, the irksome idiot is delighted with himself. Unshakably. He is immunized against self-doubt and convinced of his rights. The happy imbecile tramples your rights without a second thought. The fool takes his beliefs for truths graven in marble, whereas all true knowledge is built on sand. Uncertainty makes you crazy, certainty makes you stupid; you've got to choose your camp. The asshole thinks he knows better than you—not only does he know what you should think, feel, and do with your ten fingers, he knows how you should vote. He knows who you are and what's good for you better than you do. If you disagree with him, he will despise you, insult you, and assault you, literally and figuratively, for your own good. And if he can do that in the name of some higher ideal, he won't hesitate to attack the scum that your existence represents for him, with utter impunity.

And here's a bitter truth: justified self-defense is a trap. If you try to reason with an idiot or to change his mind, you're lost. The moment you decide it's your duty to improve him, the moment you think you know how he should think and act (like you, of course), the jig's up. There it is; now you're the idiot—and you're naïve to boot, since you think you're up to the challenge. Worse, the more you try to reform an idiot, the stronger he gets. He delights in seeing himself as a victim who annoys others—and who must for that reason be in the right. In reproving him, you allow him to believe in good faith that he's a hero of anticonformity, someone who ought to be defended and admired. A member of the resistance . . . Tremble before the vastness of this curse: if you try to reform a moron, not only will you fail, you will also strengthen him and encourage imitators. Before, there was only one moron: now there are two. Fighting against stupidity only makes it stronger. The more you attack an ogre, the more souls he devours.

The Horsefeathers of the Apocalypse

Thus, there is no way that stupidity can lose its power. It's exponential. Are we living today—more so than yesterday and less so than tomorrow—in the golden age of idiocy? As far back as the written record extends, the greatest minds of their ages believed this to be the case. Maybe they were right, at the time. Then again, maybe, like everyone else, they were just old fools. Nonetheless, the novelty of the contemporary era is that it would take only one idiot with a red button to eradicate all stupidity, and the whole world with it. An idiot elected by sheep who were only too proud to choose their slaughterer.

The other great characteristic of our age is that, even if we admit that stupidity has not yet reached its pinnacle, we know that it has never before been so visible, so unabashed, so outspoken, and so peremptory. It's enough to make you despair of your benighted fellow man. On the other hand—who knows?—it might inspire you to turn to philosophy to address the situation, given how hard it is of late to deny the vanity of everything and the narcissism of everyone, not to mention the inanity of appearances and the prevalence of sweeping judgments. If only a second Erasmus would write us a new *In Praise of Folly* (but in 280-character bursts, to save us from migraines)! If only a new Lucretius would arise to bring us relief, and perhaps joy—which we could relish, safe on shore, as the ship of fools sinks in the swirl, sabotaged by its passengers, who cry for help as they drown. Like a greedy gourmand, we lick our lips at the prospect of that desirable nectar: the war of fools among themselves, hackles raised, egos cocked. Great minds think alike, small minds collide. As you struggle to remain a spectator, not an actor, in this battle scene, it would be foolhardy to imagine yourself less vulnerable to stupidity than your bitter, braying, miserable, agitated contemporaries. But if by chance you turn out to be right, what a victory! It's wiser to be modest; if you try to rise above the throng you won't be forgiven. Escape from the herd and you'll still be led to the slaughterhouse. Howl with the wolves, bleat with the sheep, but never go it alone; everyone will cry foul. Needless to say, if you truly believe yourself to be smarter and more admirable than the average joe, the fateful diagnosis is near at hand: you yourself are most likely an unwitting carrier of stupidity.

Given the immensity of the catastrophe, the project of this book, which is to attempt to investigate stupidity, can hardly be anything but another act of folly. To tackle such a subject is to reveal yourself to be presumptuous, touchingly naïve, or at the very least, exceedingly foolish. I know this very well, but it's time that a brave idiot entered the breach. With a little luck, this endeavor will prove merely ridiculous. And ridicule is not fatal. But stupidity is! And it will outlast us. At any rate, it will bury us. That is, unless it follows us into the grave. . . .

One final point: these reflections on fools are not restricted to the male of the species. Let female fools take comfort! Neither sex has a monopoly on stupidity. And so I proclaim, O idiots of every stripe and morons of all kinds—blowhards and bitches, genial dumbasses and silly twats; dirty bastards and nasty ballbreakers, pathetic ninnies and evil louts, dunces and ditzes, oafs and space cadets, poor slobs and dizzy dames, lunkheads and airheads, scatterbrains and dingbats, lummoxes and nitwits, imbeciles, boobies, numbskulls, dolts, wastes of space, blockheads, zeros, clowns, dummies, dim bulbs, raging assholes, and empty-headed rubes, dickheads, pipsqueaks, lowlifes, daydreamers, mouth-breathers, pains in the ass, and motormouths—this is your moment of glory: this book speaks only to you. But you will not recognize yourselves. . . .

Your devoted dumbass,
Jean-François Marmion

THE SCIENTIFIC
STUDY OF IDIOTS

❧

> Serge Ciccotti ‹

Psychologist and researcher at the
University of Southern Brittany

The ignorant man affirms, the scientist doubts,
the wise man reflects.

—ARISTOTLE

s it possible to make a scientific study of idiots? It's a provocative question! We know of asinine studies (for example: "Farting as a Defense Against Unspeakable Dread"[1]), and studies on pointless jobs that have no social value and bring little personal satisfaction;[2] but studies on idiots themselves? What would that even look like?

Actually, if you look at the scientific literature in the psychological domain, you'll find that bullshit, in a general way, has been fairly well researched. In this sense, you could say that, yes, it's possible to conduct a scientific investigation of idiots; but in so doing, it's important to recognize that the study of idiots is no more or less than the study of all mankind. A portrait of the idiot can be drawn from some of the variables that different studies have explored. This will allow us to gain a relatively precise idea of the idiot (interfering, stupid, rather limited in attention span or intellect), and of some of their variations, such as the conceited, brutal blowhard, whose stupidity contains an element of toxic narcissism, not to mention a total lack of empathy.

Stupidity and the Short Attention Span

Rather than study the idiot as an object, psychological research focuses on understanding *why* people act like idiots sometimes.

Studies of behavioral scripts[3] show that most of the time people do not analyze their environment deeply before they act. They depend on familiar, habitual routine actions, which they execute automatically in response to internal or environmental factors. That's why, if you happen to be crying, there's always some moron standing by who says, "Hey, how are you doing?" That's as stupid as checking your watch a second time, right after you've just looked at it.

When you want to know what time it is, you look at your watch. The script unfolds mechanically. This mechanism allows you to be inattentive, because the effect of the script is to reduce the amount of attention required to complete a task. Consequently, because you're not paying attention and are thinking of other things, you look at your watch without seeing it. The information is not retained; which is why you have to look again to check the time. It's stupid, isn't it?

In the field of research on attentional resources, psychologists have demonstrated that people often are blind to change,[4] and that even an important alteration is not always perceived by the individual. That's why, if you've lost fifteen pounds on a diet, you always run into some asshole who doesn't see the difference. Research on the illusion of control[5] allows us to understand why, for instance, you'll always find some jerk pressing the elevator button like a maniac when it's already been pressed. Studies on social influence show that when a moronic driver goes down a dead-end street, some idiot always follows him; and when you ask a contestant on a quiz show if it's the sun or the moon that revolves around the Earth, the moron asks to poll the audience.

Human beings tend to cast aside pure reason and expected values. The dumbest among us, as a rule, is the one whose outlook reflects the greatest divergence from the average of studied effects. Generally, his vision of the world is simplistic: he has trouble with large numbers, with square roots, with complexity, and indeed with the bell curve itself, where he is to be found on the fringes. Stalin once said, "The death of one man is a tragedy; the death of millions is a statistic." As a rule, people are more receptive to anecdotes than to scientific reports stuffed with figures. But the idiot devours anecdotes. He will know someone who fell forty floors and didn't get a scratch ... anyway, "that's what I heard on the news."

Stupidity and Faith

Studies of belief show that people have faith in justice ("Belief in a Just World"[6]), which is probably the most common shared belief on earth. The worst assholes illustrate how this belief can be misused when they say things like: "Sure, she was raped, but did you see how she was dressed?" The dumber a person is, the more likely he is to blame the victim. Another sort of asshole will deride the poor as "filthy beggars."

Idiots excel in their capacity to believe anything and everything, from folktales to conspiracy theories, from the moon's influence on behavior to the effectiveness of homeopathy (it works on the dog, there's proof!). On May 28, 2017, a motorcycle was filmed driving several miles on the highway without its driver, who had fallen off. Some confirmed idiots attributed this phenomenon to the supernatural specter known as the "woman in white"; brainier types put it down to gyroscopic effect.[7] There seems to be a negative correlation between holding mystical beliefs and winning a Nobel Prize.[8]

Studies[9] in the realm of belief always distinguish between the naïve credulity of greenhorns and the entrenched stupidity of old fools.[10] It's been proven that negative memories fade with time, whereas positive memories endure. This is why the older a person gets, the greater his tendency to regard the past in a positive light, which is why old fools like to complain wistfully, "Everything was better in the good old days."

A large swath of irrational human behavior has been scrutinized by psychologists, who have determined that it springs from the individual's need to control his environment. Every living organism expresses this need (think of how your dog races to the door every time the bell rings, even though it's never for him). This compulsion can result in absurd actions by members of the human species, like, for instance, going to see a psychic. There are about a hundred thousand people in France who declare themselves to be "psychics"; they earn more than $3 billion a year. Researchers have never identified any genuine gift in self-styled psychics, but that doesn't keep these so-called seers from benefiting their clients. It's estimated that 20 percent of women and 10 percent of men have consulted a psychic at least once in their lives. Generally, psychics report that they don't regret having chosen this fraudulent line of work to earn their crust; apparently, idiots making other idiots the basis of their livelihood works perfectly well as a business model. The need for control is often accompanied by the illusion of control; and idiots probably delude themselves that they are in control more than others.[11] One proof of the power of this illusion can be shown through the everyday example of driving or riding in a car. When you're a passenger, you fear accidents much more than you do when you are the driver. There are some fools who find it impossible to sleep when they are passengers; apparently they can sleep only when they're the driver!

The idiot will throw the dice as hard as he can to get sixes; he will choose his own numbers in the lottery. He will stoop to pick up a penny for luck and make sure to avoid walking under ladders. The fool has everything under control: if he wins the lottery, it's because he dreamed of the number 6 for six nights in a row, and because $6 \times 6 = 36$, he played the 36 and won. By the same token, it must be accepted that the idiot is in good mental health overall; because the illusion of control is much weaker among depressed people.[12]

Studies About Idiots That Help Explain Your Job

In another area studied widely by scientists, idiots have been found to employ an exceptionally wide range of strategies to shore up their self-esteem. Studies on bias and false consensus[13] demonstrate that people tend to exaggerate the number of other people who share their faults. This is why, when you point out to some jerk that he has blown past a stop sign, he will retort, "But nobody stops at this sign!"

The typical asshole often indulges in retrospective bias. At the maternity hospital, he'll say, "I was sure it was going to be a boy." As he stands in front of the television on election night, he'll declare, "I was sure Trump was going to be president," and sometimes when you're talking with him he'll tell you, "I knew you were going to say that!" Is the idiot showing bad faith? Is the idiot a fortune-teller? Not at all: the idiot deploys "I knew it" to strategic ends, to demonstrate that he's better informed than he really is. "I know, I know...." Of course, you must never mention these studies to idiots, as they will deny that they do such things.

To protect their self-esteem, many people overestimate their abilities. This bias has been proved by psychological experiments that demonstrate that, in multiple arenas, a large number of participants rate themselves higher than average in such categories as, for instance, intelligence and everything connected with it. On one side of the axis, you have those humble souls whose human qualities of simplicity, humility, and discretion lead others to perceive them as simpleminded or naïve, and to criticize them for lack of confidence and treat them like dummies who can be easily manipulated. On the other side of the axis, you find the high achievers, which is to say, overconfident idiots. One of these smug morons can exact a high price on society when he (for example) gets lost at sea, or gets stranded in the mountains after off-piste skiing—even if he mostly contents himself with exaggerating his prowess at maintaining speed on the highway.

Another form of bias, egocentric bias,[14] permits us to distinguish minor-league imbeciles from the gigantic assholes who don't acknowledge their own role in stupidity. The jerk who's been divorced three times because all three of the women he married were bitches, the blowhard whose business failed because he was working with a bunch of losers. Even when he was a teenager, he claimed that it wasn't his feet that stank, it was his socks. One day he was stopped in his car for speeding; that was just bad luck. He can't understand that luck is the spin that assholes put on probability.

The researchers David Dunning and Justin Kruger could not have published an article with a title like "Studies About Idiots That Help Explain Your Job." If they had presented their work that way it never would have made it through peer review at a scientific journal. Yet in their research, this is what they abundantly demonstrated. These two specialists discovered that incompetent people tend to overestimate their own level of competence. That is why a fool who's never had a dog will tell you how to train yours. Dunning and Kruger attribute this tendency to the difficulty that unqualified people have, in certain contexts, with assessing their true abilities. But that's not all: according to these psychologists,[15] not only does the incompetent person overestimate his own level of competence, he also fails to recognize competence in those who possess it.

Thanks to their research, we can understand why a stupid client will tell a professional how to do his job, and why when you lose something some moron is bound to say to you, "Wait, where was it the last time you saw it?" It also explains why a fool will feel compelled to say, "It's easy to be a lawyer, law is top-of-the-head stuff"; "Quitting smoking? It's just a question of willpower"; "Flying an airplane? It's like driving a bus"; and so on. This is why when an idiot strolls out of a lecture on quantum physics of which he has not understood a single word, he will feel free to look the expert straight in the eyes and say: "Could be, could be . . ."

Dunning and Kruger suggest that if we were prudent we would be tempted not to vote in elections. Given how useless we are at economy, geopolitics, and running major institutions, we are incapable of evaluating electoral platforms or of having any idea how to improve the country's direction. All the same, any idiot at a bar will say, "I know how to solve the crisis!" A number of studies conducted with Asian participants display an inverse Dunning-Kruger effect;[16] in other words, they underestimate their abilities. It appears that in the culture of the Far East, where the prevailing norm is to avoid standing out, the desire to prove that you've mastered every subject does not exist.

Bullshit Detector

Even though many more mechanisms could be included here to help us define stupidity, let's wrap up this short synthesis with a discussion of cynical mistrust, a quality in which the idiot and the asshole are more deeply steeped than other people.[17] Cynicism is defined as a collection of negative beliefs about human nature and its motivations. The asshole is often prey to sociopolitical cynicism—just ask him. A few phrases punctuate his running commentary: "They're all corrupt"; "A bunch of crooks and losers"; "Psychologists? Charlatans, every last one of them"; "Journalists? Bootlickers." They think that people who act honestly do so only out of fear of being caught.

The asshole lives in a world of incompetence and deceit. Studies show that cynical idiots are so uncooperative and mistrustful that they miss out on professional opportunities, and therefore earn less than others do.

In sum, the idiot embodies a sort of exaggerated version of the various tendencies the researchers observed. An idiot who manages to accumulate all these tendencies will become the "emperor of idiots," which is to say, the most gigantic asshole the earth has ever seen.

But the key question, tied to our starting point—"Is it possible to make a scientific study of idiots?"—is probably: "Why are there so *many* idiots?" Because it is undeniably true that there are. If you shout "poor bastard" in the street, every head will turn around. Once again, the scientific literature provides the answer; indeed, many answers.

First of all, we're all equipped with a bullshit detector called negativity bias.[18] This is a tendency that leads us to give more weight, attention, and interest to negative things than to positive ones. Negativity bias has significant consequences on people's opinions, on their prejudices and stereotypes, on discrimination and superstition. As with housework, we notice the little things only when they *haven't* been done. It's because of our negativity bias that we find it easier to deal with an idiot than with a genius in a complex social setting. In addition, this bias leads us to read more meaning into a negative event than a positive one. If you're looking for something that you've lost at home, your reflex is to think that you didn't lose it, someone else must have put it somewhere. "Who took my . . . ?" Ultimately, when anything fails, there's a tendency to think that there's a reason for it, that some idiot must have wrecked everything.

And finally, let's note that researchers have discovered a fundamental distortion in the attribution process.[19] When you observe someone, you attribute their behavior to deep-dyed character, as opposed to any external factors that may be relevant. In many cases, you come to the natural conclusion: the guy's an idiot. As a result, when a car zooms past us, it must be because the driver is a brute, and not because one of his kids got hurt at school; when a friend doesn't answer an email for two hours it's because he's angry, not because he had an internet outage. If a colleague hasn't handed in a file yet, it's because he's lazy, not because he's overworked; if a professor responds to me curtly it's because he's a jerk, not because my question was stupid. This mechanism increases our tendency to spot idiots everywhere. Those are at least two of the reasons why we are so sensitive to stupidity.

A TAXONOMY
OF MORONS

› Jean-François Dortier ‹

Founder and editorial director of the magazines
Le Cercle Psy [Psychological Circle] *and* Sciences
Humaines [Social Sciences]

f there are multiple forms of intelligence, as psychologists assert, it stands to reason that there must also be an impressive range of forms of stupidity. Given the embryonic stage of development of this science (to which this book adds a few important milestones) and the dearth of authoritative studies, we should begin with an overview of representative samples.

Backwardness

Backward, slow, ignorant, idiotic, useless, foolish, lug-headed, imbecilic, stupid, witless, cracked, silly, moronic, dippy . . . the vocabulary of stupidity is endless. These semantic riches reflect subtle gradations in meaning, variation in usage, and the effects of social trends.

On the whole, however, the meaning always comes down to the same thing: whatever the variety of epithets and metaphors, the fool is a person who is judged to be of reduced intelligence and limited mental scope. Thus, stupidity is always defined invidiously, as a relative concept. A person is not inherently stupid (if everyone was stupid, nobody would notice it). Put another way, stupidity is measured from a fixed point established by a person who considers himself superior.

Rubes

Also known as rednecks or hillbillies, rubes are stupid, cruel, racist, and selfish. At least that's how the French satirist Cabu, who immortalized their traits in his comic strips, depicted them. They dominate the ranks of the voters who elect populist parties, because they're stupid; which is to say they're incapable of political probity, and they rely on short-term logic and sweeping generalizations. Their thinking is categorical—everything is black or white, with no nuance. They're stubborn and obtuse, and rational arguments hold no sway with them: they won't ever back down from their opinions. They think what they think, period.

They're cruel because, lacking any empathy, they seek out scapegoats and lash out at innocent victims like Arabs, blacks, and migrants in general.

They're selfish because only one thing matters to them: their well-being and comfort; their pocketbook.

But do these rubes conform to an actual psychological profile? If this were the case it would be necessary to demonstrate an organic relationship between stupidity (in the sense of a low level of intellect) and cruelty (defined as selfishness combined with contempt for others).

And yet, the link between these two qualities is only conjectural: a person can be stupid and kind (consider the "village idiot"), just as a person can be intelligent and cruel. Is that not the case of the caricaturists Cabu and Jean-Marc Reiser, who worked for a magazine called *Hara-Kiri*, whose motto was "stupid and nasty"? Those men were not truly stupid (even if the systematic use of caricature and cliché ultimately produces a deadening effect on the wit). Nasty: that they often were.

The Universal Idiot

"They're all morons!" This phrase is uttered, usually rather loudly, by someone sitting on a barstool. But who is this "they"? Politicians, the voters who elect them, bureaucrats, incompetents, and by extension, pretty much everybody—since the phrase does not carry a lot of nuance.

This absence of discernment in analysis, this arrogance that places itself above the common run of humanity to levy judgment on the rest of the world: these are almost foolproof signs that you're dealing with a true idiot. "The peculiar nature of error is that it does not recognize itself," Descartes observed. This is especially true of stupidity. Obviously, a fool cannot recognize himself. On the contrary, he himself constitutes a kind of lightning rod of folly. Wherever you happen to be, if you hear someone declare "They're all morons!" you can be sure that there's a moron in the vicinity.

Artificial Stupidity

"Computers are totally stupid."[1] This assertion doesn't come from just anyone. Gérard Berry teaches computer science at the Collège de France. A specialist in artificial intelligence, he does not hesitate to challenge the speculations (ill-informed) on the capacity of machines to surpass human intelligence.

Certainly, artificial intelligence has made significant progress in the last sixty years. And certainly, machines can recognize images, translate texts, and produce medical diagnoses. In 2016, the Deepmind computer program AlphaGo succeeded in defeating one of the world's best players of Go, the Japanese game of strategy. While this performance was impressive, we should not overlook the fact that AlphaGo knows how to do only one thing: to play the game of Go. The same was true of the Deep Blue program that beat Garry Kasparov at chess in 1996, more than twenty years ago. All that these so-called intelligent machines do is develop an extremely specialized competence, which is taught to them by their human master. Speculations on the autonomy of machines that can "learn on their own" are nothing but myths. Machines don't know how to transfer skills acquired from one domain into another; whereas one of the basic mechanisms of human intelligence is analogical transfer. The strength of computers is the power of their memories to retain the work they've done, and their electrifying capacity for calculation.

"Learning machines" that work on the principle of "deep

learning" (the new generation of artificial intelligence) are not intelligent, because they don't understand what they're doing. All that Google's automatic translation program does, for instance, is learn how to use a word in a given context (drawing on an immense reservoir of examples); but it remains perfectly "stupid" in the process. In no case does it understand the meaning of the words it uses.

This is why Gérard Berry feels justified in saying that, at root, "the computer is completely stupid."

Collective Stupidity

Collective intelligence designates a form of group intelligence, as displayed by ants, or neurons, for example. Each element in isolation is not capable of much; but as a group can produce great feats. By the magic of self-organization, ants are able to build hallways, bridal chambers, pantries, hatcheries, and ventilation systems in their anthills. Some of them practice agriculture (growing mushrooms), animal husbandry (raising aphids), etc.

Even though its functioning remains unexplained, collective intelligence has become a respected model in a very short time, resting on the simple idea that the whole is greater than the sum of its parts. Collective decision making and cocreation are better than individual decisions.

Nonetheless, it sometimes happens that the many make a worse decision than the individual. Collective intelligence has its counterpart: collective stupidity. In groups, our capacity for good judgment can be severely reduced. In his studies on group norms, the psychologist Solomon Asch long ago addressed many well-known instances of this phenomenon. To name one: if a majority of people embraces a manifestly false and idiotic theory, others will go along with it merely because of the power of conformity. To name another instance: the false virtues of brainstorming. Take a group of ten people and make them work together for half an hour on a project (like tourism slogans to promote a town, for example). At the same time, set another group to work in which each member works separately on the task. Gather up their reports: the proposals of the second group are much richer and more plentiful than the proposals of the first group. Put another way, sometimes the whole is less than the sum of its parts.

It would be beside the point to conduct large-scale psychological experiments to investigate collective folly. Everything that could be proven in the lab is experienced every day in offices, where collective efforts in meetings produce so many stupid ideas that it's hard not to think that one foolish person had dreamed them all up on his own.

Gullibility

What could be more gullible than a child? You can make a kid believe almost anything: that there's an old guy with a white beard somewhere up in the sky who travels in a flying sled pulled by reindeer, delivering gifts to good children; or that a little fairy hunts under pillows for baby teeth, which she replaces with a quarter when she finds one. . . .

Gullibility is a form of stupidity that is altogether appropriate to childhood. That, in any case, is what the psychologist Jean Piaget thought. The philosopher Lucien Lévy-Bruhl thought that "primitive peoples" were very credulous, too, because of their animist beliefs in "forest spirits" endowed with magical powers, which proved, he thought, that the "savages," like children, had not attained the age of reason.

But with the advance of scientific research, it has become necessary to concede that children were not as naïve as people thought: they accept that reindeer can fly, but only in a parallel universe that does not obey the laws that apply down here, where they know very well that reindeer can't fly. We ourselves, rational adults, are prepared to believe in the existence of particles that exhibit strange behaviors (the ubiquitous miracle of long-distance communication) without any confirmation from experts. Some of these scientists are people of faith, some of them even believe in the Resurrection of Christ.

These realizations have led psychologists and sociologists to take another look at what it means to be gullible. Gullibility can no longer be seen to reflect a lack of logic (in other words, infantile stupidity). Believing in things that appear to be unbelievable is related to a system of reference, rather than to naïveté or to an absence of discernment.

At the end of his life, Lucien Lévy-Bruhl admitted that he had been mistaken about the mentality of the "primitives." It's to his credit that he acknowledged his error, a pretty rare occurrence in the world of philosophers.

Slowness

When, at the end of the nineteenth century, Jules Ferry made primary education obligatory in France, it appeared that certain students were incapable of absorbing routine instruction. Two psychologists, Alfred Binet and Theodore Simon, were asked to create an intelligence test in order to identify such children so that they could receive an adapted education. This test formed the basis of what would later become the famous "IQ"—the Intelligence Quotient.

By convention, the average IQ of a population is 100 percent. The emergence of the IQ tests led to the definition of mental deficiency and its subtypes: from "borderline deficiency," among those whose IQ was less than 80 (and higher than 65); to "moderate deficiency," applying to those who scored between 50 and 65; to "profound deficiency" (members of this category were once deemed "imbeciles"), with an IQ of 20 to 34. Still further below, with an IQ inferior to 20, are the "profoundly backward" (formerly classified as "idiots").

Today, the words "retarded" and "impaired" are out of favor in psychology; they have been replaced by euphemisms. We speak of "learning disabilities" and we avoid the expressions "handicapped" and "differently abled." In the same way, we no longer speak of "geniuses" or "gifted" children; we speak of "precocious children" or of children with "high potential." This doesn't keep anyone, in practice, from using tests to classify children according to their degree of mental disability, so they can be guided to specialized methods of instruction.

Imbecile, Idiot

At the dawn of psychiatry, the terms "imbecility" and "idiocy" were used to describe people who displayed a very low level of intellect, who could not read, write, and in certain cases, speak. Philippe Pinel, the French physician who is sometimes called the "father of modern psychiatry," considered Victor de l'Aveyron (better known as the "wild boy of Aveyron") to be an "idiot." Today the boy would be classified as autistic. In the words of the psychiatrist Jean-Étienne Esquirol, "The idiot is an individual who knows nothing, is capable of nothing, and wants nothing. Every idiot embodies, more or less, the acme of incapacity."

Dr. Paul Sollier, in his 1891 book *Psychologie de l'Idiot et de l'Imbécile: Essai de Psychologie Morbide* [*The Psychology of the Idiot and the Imbecile: An Essay on Psychological Morbidity*], devoted one chapter to "idiots and imbeciles." Apologizing for the tardy progress of French psychology, as compared to English and American achievement in the science, he noted that there was no consensus on the right way to define idiocy or imbecility: some use intelligence as the evaluative factor, others rely on language (the inability to speak correctly); still others apply moral considerations (a lack of self-control).

Over time, psychologists would abandon the concept of the "idiot." The only remnant of this notion that still pops up on occasion is the term "idiot savant," though even there, the term "savant syndrome" is preferred. The profile, which incorporates certain cases of autism and of the developmental disorder known as Williams syndrome, is marked by deficits in language or in general intelligence, and also by unusual difficulties with mathematics, drawing, and music.

For centuries, the village idiot was the archetype of a intellectually disabled person, the fool, the simpleton. Not too long ago, every village had its "crackpot" (*fada* is the expression used in the south of France), who would be hired for menial tasks. This oaf was regarded as pleasant and harmless, always smiling and happy, laughing over nothing. He wasn't considered dangerous. In *Snow White and the Seven Dwarfs*, Dopey, with his beatific smile, big eyes, and crooked cap, illustrates the type.

Loons

"Loon" is a cute way to talk about fools, not angry fools, but the dreamy kind caught up in a fantasy world. The loon is a step away from the weirdo—that is to say, a loon who does bizarre or excessive things. And the weirdo is not far removed from the freak, who, according to the rigorous National Center for Textual and Lexical Resources, is "generally a fantasist who displays eccentric behavior." In current French usage, the expression "freak out" can mean horse around, show off, or act goofy; and it also approximates the French expression *"faire le zouave"*: to act like a clown. In English, "get your freak on" recently entered the *Oxford English Dictionary*, meaning, roughly, to engage in uninhibited sexual behavior, or to dance like a maniac.

A THEORY OF ASSHOLES

A Conversation with
> Aaron James <

Professor of philosophy at the University of California,
Irvine, and author of Assholes: A Theory

science, culture, and politics. He had taught physics and mathematics for many years in various institutions. He preached that physicists like Albert Einstein, Ernst Mach, Edwin Hubble, Fred Hoyle, "and many others" had proved that, as it says in the Bible, the sun and all the planets revolve around the Earth, which is fixed in space, immobile and immutable. He nourished the hope that people would give Scripture its rightful place and understand that science wasn't what it was cracked up to be.

Yet every new scientific discovery brings new proof that geocentrism does not correspond to reality. Exponents of geocentrism have nothing to back them up but the Bible. To every scientific argument they respond: "It says in the Bible that . . ." Attacking Galileo tarnishes the image of one of the founders of modern science, who conducted one of the first proofs of Copernicus's heliocentrism, and it also scrubs away what some consider to be the blot caused by the Catholic Church's apology in 1992 for the condemnation of Galileo.

There's been plenty of water under the bridge since Galileo. Copernican science had to take on Scripture and the belief in God's Revealed Truth, and to wage war on the irrational. Scientists were persecuted. Today some reductionists and crackpots are trying to manipulate minds so they can pass along their hazy theories: the battle of obscurantism against the truth continues.

Can Anything Defeat Obscurantism?

While it's unlikely that anyone can increase their intelligence, with proper application of method it is possible to learn how to develop your critical thinking.

Not all beliefs are stupid, absurd, or dangerous. Certain beliefs are constructive, like belief in oneself and in one's capacities, in self-worth, in life, and in one another.

The risk of our being so influenced by dangerous beliefs that we lose our reason comes from the need to find meaning in life, whatever the cost. When other people transmit an explanation that corresponds to our vision of the world, or that removes our need to search for it ourselves, it can be easy to adopt it.

But what makes irrational beliefs so powerful is their tendency to mesh with our intuitive expectations.

From the beginning of time, many people have believed bizarre things, and many people have struggled to fight against those beliefs. This creates an equilibrium that, over time, doesn't really change. In this way, you can fight for reason with the understanding that you're simply participating in a balancing act.

As intelligent, cultured, and critical as a person may be, no human being is entirely free from some absurd belief, essentially because it's so difficult to accept the role of chance. Looking to destiny, fate, conspiracy, plots, and good or bad intentions to explain luck is a universal bias. "Lightning doesn't strike twice," "Where there's smoke, there's fire," and "Good things come to those who wait" are all expressions that demonstrate our need for causality and meaning. The greatest scientists could not avoid it. That's why Einstein wrote in his letters about the illness of his wife, Mileva, and their son: "Well-deserved punishment for my having taken the most important step of my life so rashly. I begot children with a physically and morally inferior person."[5]

Einstein's mother had tried to dissuade him from marrying Mileva, who had a limp, predicting that his children would be affected. You might have expected more broad-mindedness from the inventor of the theory of relativity! But as two of his biographers, Roger Highfield and Paul Carter, have said, Einstein "was a man whose combination of intellectual vision and emotional myopia left behind him a series of damaged lives."

At root, perhaps what lies in our power is not to make fewer people believe bizarre or crazy things, but to make sure there are not more people who fall prey to them. It's very rare that anyone can succeed in changing the opinions of those who are already convinced of them. The risk is rather that by challenging them, you reinforce their beliefs.

WHY WE FIND MEANING IN COINCIDENCES

⁓

A Conversation with
› Nicolas Gauvrit ‹

*Psychologist and mathematician, professor at l'ESPE
Lille-Nord-de-France, institutional member of the university
laboratory Cognitions Humaine et Artificielle (CHArt)*

Q. Certain coincidences seem so stupefying that we refuse to attribute them to chance, and look for meaning in them. But you put this down to a faulty perception of context.

A. Our vision is localized, fixed in time and space. If you look at it from a global perspective, coincidences aren't that shocking. And furthermore, for the most part, we don't ask the right questions. Take the paradox of birthdays: in a group of twenty-five people, what's the likelihood that two of them have the same birth date? In answering the question, we're tempted to rely on a heuristic, a simplified form of reasoning, and ask ourselves what the probability is that, among twenty-five people, one would share our own birthday.

The result is pretty weak, because we reduce the problem to only one possible date, our own birth date. The probability that one person in twenty-five would have the same birth date as me is only 6.3 percent. And yet, the chance that two people in a group of twenty-five would have the same birthday is one in two. But that's not at all the same question.

Q. You give the example of a woman, Violet Jessop, who survived three shipwrecks, including the *Titanic*. That may

seem extraordinary, but at the end of the day, it isn't, not at all.

A. The problem derives from the fact that we have insufficient information, and we fill in the gaps with default elements that seem probable and implicit. When we hear without any further details that someone has survived the wreck of the *Titanic* and two other shipwrecks, we imagine that the other two wrecks were comparable to the *Titanic*, which isn't at all the case, since one of them had very few victims, and the other had none at all. Moreover, you assume that there's nothing particularly unique about Violet Jessop. But she worked for the companies of all three of those ships.

Q. **You also say that, in attempts to "decode" the events of September 11, the number 11 pops up a lot, which produces the temptation to see conspiracy or the hand of fate. But you see nothing extraordinary in it.**

A. This applies to all numerology and fetish numbers. The number 19, for example, appears hundreds of times in the Koran, and the number 7 in the Bible—or in any case, multiples of it—which is hardly astonishing, statistically speaking.

You can also find predictions in word form, in the Bible for instance—a supposedly secret code. A few years ago, in his book *The Bible Code*, the journalist Michael Drosnin used a variety of reading grids to reveal all sorts of predictions, including the end of the world. In reality, the number of possible grids and computer analyses you could apply to the text is so enormous that you could find absolutely anything. Drosnin even issued a challenge: see if you can find as many predictions in *Moby-Dick* as in the Bible. Well ... it had already been done!

Besides, in the Bible, applying the same technique, people have also found passages that say "God doesn't exist," and "Hate Jesus." As with anything else, you can find what you want.

Q. Including in your own book?[1]

A. Definitely! In Pascal's *Pensées*, I found a prediction of thousands of deaths from AIDS. Sébastien Pommier, a computer scientist, found the words "chicken and french fries" in the genome of beer yeast, when he alphabetically encoded it. Which was what he'd had for lunch. ...

If you apply one reading grid chosen at random, the probability of finding "chicken and French fries" is very low, but if you multiply that by a very large number of different grids, it's another thing entirely.

Q. You've calculated that, over the last twenty years, seventy-two thousand premonitory dreams might have genuinely predicted the death of someone the following week but would have gone unnoticed.

A. Yes, that's just an estimate, but it's one more illustration of the conjunction of weak probability with a large sampling. Henri Broch made a similar calculation for a television program on mystery, during which a medium asked the television audience to turn on the lights in their homes, so he could make lightbulbs shatter all across France. People phoned in by the dozens, aghast, to affirm that a lightbulb really had burst in their homes. Incredible! But given that the program lasted an hour, and supposing that every viewer had four or five lightbulbs, it was predictable that a few hundred would burn out during the program, given the average life span of a lightbulb. The probability was very weak for each lamp, but elevated for hundreds of thousands of them.

Q. **He might just as well have pretended to cause births and deaths!**

A. Yes, but people know that things like that happen often. People don't normally talk about lightbulbs exploding. The same applies to premonitory dreams. I've had quite a few myself, violent ones, which seemed real, but luckily, turned out not to be. Otherwise, I'd have two friends less at the very least. . . .

Q. **Why is it that not one single prediction of astrologists or clairvoyants ever comes true, that there's never a coincidence?**

A. Oh, but predictions regularly come true. Elizabeth Teissier had foreseen that something would happen in September 2001. Not an attack, and not on the eleventh, but still . . . In general, their predictions are more foreseeable—earthquakes, accidents. But not September 11, which was truly unexpected. Elizabeth Teissier, to justify her predictions, often declares that she foresaw airplane accidents. For fun, someone started using the computer to generate random predictions, and that turned out to be more effective, a bit, than Elizabeth Teissier. This remains a problem with anniversaries: if you make a list of dates on which accidents will occur, it's not improbable that you'll end up with one or two coincidences.

Q. **You attack certain psychological approaches, like psycho-genealogy[2] and synchronicity.**

A. Psychogenealogy, essentially, is based on coincidences between the dates of significant events in our own lives and events that happened to our ancestors. In essence, it's a slightly more complicated variation on the birthday paradox, because this time we're looking for coincidences between two distinct lists. But once you start constructing an enriched, expanded genealogical tree, it's not rare to find yourself with hundreds of dates, which heightens the prob-ability of a coincidence. Furthermore, in practice, people don't really have exact dates. In the worst case, when people really find *nothing*, they find a way to make up a connection.

One twenty-four-year-old patient had a great uncle who died at thirty, while traveling. A psychologist came up with a connection, telling the man that he was in a dynamic to kick off at around thirty. How funny. And yes, I'm also regularly asked about the concept of synchronicity.[3] Jung wanted to elaborate a theory on it, with the help of mathematicians and a physicist, but it never came to anything.

Q. Nevertheless, people can't stop themselves from assigning meaning to coincidences. I suppose you yourself might be tempted, in spite of everything.

A. Absolutely! An event with a weak probability seems much more astonishing to us when it happens to us than when it happens to other people. Recently I was testing children on their perception of luck, by throwing a die behind a barrier, and asking them to guess eight times in a row what number would come up. I wanted to analyze the sequences of predictions they produced. Out of seventy children, one succeeded four times in a row. At the end of these attempts, I told myself: "This is terrible, if this can happen, I must be wrong, premonition does exist!" I had to reason with myself: one out of seventy, that can be explained by chance. It's like optical illusions. You fall for them in the moment, but you can reason your way out of them.

There's a phenomenon called the "Clustering Illusion," related to "excessive expectation of randomness." That is to say, you expect chance to reflect the ideas you have of it. To be more specific, you expect that dates chosen at random will not be ordered in any special grouping but will be uniformly dispersed. In reality, when you choose twelve dates at random, two will fall in the same month, or even three. This excessive expectation of randomness can lead us to make mistakes, but it's not irrational.

Q. Does that mean there's a tendency to believe that chance itself must obey certain rules?

A. Actually, it's true that when you take into consideration both time—because you don't wait for the random dates to occur—and space, you imagine the selected events as if spread out across a surface, far apart from each other. The aerial bombardments of London during the Second World War serve as a good historic example. The German aviators flew so high over the clouds that they couldn't see where the bombs were going, so they fell totally randomly. But when the British government looked at the map of the impacts, they could see that the bombs were concentrated in certain points that corresponded to no obvious military objective. They deduced that the Germans had bad maps. In reality, a statistical analysis showed that the targets weren't really chosen, they were randomly dispersed.

Q. Paradoxically, you explain that there's no doubt we owe the survival of our species to these cognitive illusions: it's better to see too many coincidences than too few.

A. Evolutionary psychologists suggest that we've been conditioned to detect them. In an era when it could be a question of life or death, it was better to overinterpret coincidences and run away as soon as the leaves started rustling—which might indicate a predator—than to underestimate their importance and make no deductions.

In any case, the scientific method consists of looking for coincidences and correlations and interpreting them through some other means than chance. This isn't irrational, but it's a risky method, because it doesn't always produce reliable conclusions. For example, one *a priori* experiment, which was correctly conducted, proved the existence of a "Mozart effect," by which people became smarter when they listened to Mozart. But when they tried to replicate it, it didn't work. You've got to assume that there was a false positive, which is something that must happen a lot. Illusions like these are the flaw in the rational method.

Q. Finally, where does our resistance to chance come from? Does it have to do with some pure cognitive incapacity, or does it arise out of fear?

A. I don't think we're afraid of it, but in general, we like to have an explanation: that's why we invented science. Nevertheless, I don't really have an answer.

Interview by Jean-François Marmion.

STUPIDITY AS LOGICAL DELIRIUM

> Boris Cyrulnik ‹

Neuropsychiatrist and director of studies
at the University of Toulon

othing is more common or more serious than stupidity. Of all living creatures, we human beings are certainly the most gifted at it, given that we live in a world of representations, some of which, despite their coherence and their internal logic, reveal themselves to be totally detached from reality. We call these representations "fantasies" when they pertain to a psychotic, but for you and me, it usually comes down to simple stupidity. It's very easy to find thousands of examples of it in all spheres of human intelligence.

Take the biological realm. If I claim that the psychopharmacological effect of taking two doses of vitamin B_6 is exactly equivalent to taking one dose of vitamin B_{12}, mathematical logic will allow me to lull you into believing that this makes perfect sense. But adapted to another realm, this logic can be stupid. To demonstrate this, I performed a small calculation inspired by the psychiatrist and psychoanalyst Wilhelm Reich. The expectation of the longevity of the sex life of a couple is about fifty years, sometimes more. At the rate of two sexual encounters per week, the typical frequency in our culture, this means five thousand to six thousand sexual encounters overall.

Yet in France, which gets the gold medal for birth rate in Europe, women give birth, on average, to 1.9 children. Schematically, this would mean one child per three thousand sexual encounters. Statistically, therefore, it's highly improbable that sexual intercourse causes pregnancy! It's unanswerable. (Let us note in passing that by this mathematical reckoning, it would take 2,399,200,000,000 acts of intercourse to obtain a population of 7.5 billion humans.)

The Perilous Leaps of "Psycholacanists"

And what do shrinks have to say about this? It's profitable here to consider the brief history of the competition between the celebrated psychoanalysts Jacques Lacan and Sigmund Freud. Lacan's jealousy was the spur to a fundamental theoretical divergence that would produce "psycholacanysis," which is to say, a form of psychoanalysis heavily influenced by Lacan's thinking and wordplay—venerated today by his admirers, who repeat his theories without a word of critique or discussion. It's worth noting, for example, that a Jewish patient once said to Lacan: "Every morning, I'm woken by anxiety. It's been this way ever since the war; it's the exact same time when the Gestapo knocked at the door." Lacan extracted himself from his armchair and his theories to perform a practical action. Stroking the woman's cheek, he spoke the words, "*Geste à peau, geste à peau,*" which in French means "a gesture with the skin"; and, more importantly, is a homonym of "Gestapo." The patient's reaction? "This is absolutely marvelous!" Whatever works. . . .

It's also worth noting that Lacan's work on the "mirror stage" of psychological development was inspired by animal ethology, a fact that he frankly admitted. He was also one of the first people who would have read a publication like this one—no matter what today's psycholacanists say, who hate me because I emphasize this connection, which can be confirmed in the blink of an eye. As far back as 1946, in his book *The First Year of Life* (which had a preface by Anna Freud), the American psychoanalyst René Spitz made twenty-eight references to animal ethology. I conclude from this that, without even having read their own seminal texts, psycholacanists attack me in the name of an idea of reality they have invented, not in the name of reality itself. This is the very definition of logical delirium.

At a conference in the 1980s, I dreamed up a hoax to illustrate what Freud called "condensation" and "displacement" in obsessional neurosis. I invented the case of a certain Otto Krank, who suffered from hysterical paralysis in both ears. He couldn't move them the way his classmates could. He went to consult a psychoanalyst or a psycholacanist, for whom the signifier was low-hanging fruit, because it had to do with a real-life situation. All that was needed, it was understood, was to change the signifier to alter the real-world effect. The psychoanalyst advised Otto to make an anagram of his first name, by writing it backward. On the following day, Otto felt much better. This cure followed the same reasoning as the "*geste à peau*": displacement, condensation, then a perilous leap.

A Few Words on the Profession

But let's be fair: stupidity can also strike just as hard on the opposite side, among therapists who embrace the scientific process. The classifications of the *Diagnostic and Statistical Manual of Mental Disorders* (*DSM*) of the American Psychiatric Association, or of the World Health Organization's *Classification Internationale des Maladies* (*CIM*), are informed by articles that have gone through peer reviews—in which I on occasion have been invited to take part. The name of the author of the research is hidden, though you often can guess who wrote the article, based on the style and the subject. Incidentally, it's altogether possible that the members of a peer review committee may include the author's brother-in-law; a friend who owes him a lot of money, or whom he's published twice, who therefore owes him a boost up the ladder; or even a nonagenarian who keeps saying the same phrase over and over ("mirror stage, mirror stage, mirror stage . . ."). In the end, this is how you build your career: by repeatedly publishing the same article, tweaking the title or altering a sentence or two, all the way up until retirement. I'm exaggerating a little, of course, but once, my friend Paul Ekman, a major pioneer of the psychology of emotions, submitted an article to a genuinely anonymous peer review, and had the article rejected by a journal that had already published it two years before. Stupidity also applies to committees that judge their friends!

It's part of the whole system, whether you're a biologist, a mathematician, a statistician, a psychoanalyst, a psycholacanist, or a clinician. It's part of the fabric of everyday life. We deserve the Nobel Prize for our indulgence! Better yet, we should get plaques in our honor on the walls of corner cafés. And yet, let us give some credit to the scientific process. It at least has the virtue of making the case for doubt, for verification, and for the acceptance of the fact that our truths are ephemeral. This must mark some kind of progress in stupidity. But if you want a scientific career, you absolutely have to prove that you're right . . . which brings us back to logical delirium. Two options are open to you: quality of career, or quality of life. If you choose the first option, you'll wage war on doubt to shore up the primacy of certainty, reinforcing both stupidity and your career prospects in the process. In this case you'll sign publications, "blah-blah-blah," to make yourself well liked, inserting the approved terms and citations. If you choose the second option, you'll flout the rules and come under attack. After a period of discomfort, you might be joined by other people to form a new faction, which, in turn, will generate its own blah-blah-blah. To think for yourself, therefore, is to doom yourself to thinking for yourself before you know if you'll be joined quickly (or not) by a band of like-minded pals to form a new band of fools. Friendly fools. With a little bit of luck, you'll have fun being idiots together. In that way, our bond with stupidity can shape our careers.

In any case, after this article appears, I suspect my own career will take a dive!

THE LANGUAGE OF STUPIDITY

› Patrick Moreau ‹

*Professor of literature at Collège Ahuntsic in Montreal,
editor in chief of Argument*

What do fools say? They themselves don't know, that's
their cover. The word of a fool, without being entirely
free of meaning, does not strive for exactitude. It's an
empty rattle, intended to banish silence. The fool . . .
attaches himself to platitudes like a drunk trapeze artist
to his safety rope. He holds on tight to the handrail of
stock phrases, and never lets go.

—GEORGES PICARD, *DE LA CONNERIE* [*ON STUPIDITY*][1]

Sometimes we do stupid things, but much more often we say them. Most of the time, they are transmitted through language. Is it possible that the lectures we dismiss as idiotic—when all they're doing is relaying a momentary lapse in intelligence—simply represent one of the multiple possible manifestations of stupidity? Is there not a specific form of stupidity, tied to language, that is the natural domain of thoughtless statements? This hypothesis approaches the Newspeak of Orwell's *1984*, which the author nicknamed "duckspeak," and which found its ideal expression "without involving the higher brain centers at all."[2]

At first glance, it may seem strange to associate everyday linguistic clumsiness with Newspeak, the canonical model for political cant of every kind. But the two forms are connected by their very nature: they both are defined by the inadequate and unconscious use of language. Stupid words, or stupid statements, as in Orwell's Newspeak, are unable to adequately assess reality. The same is true of the thoughts of those who pronounce them. Even if one of these emerges in the political and ideological arena, while the other arises spontaneously, Newspeak and everyday linguistic clumsiness have this in common: they both represent perversions of the normal and legitimate use of language and words.

Moreover, you can make the hypothesis that these two associated phenomena, initially distinct, are currently drawing nearer to each other, because of at least two concomitant factors. For one, ideologies (feminism, differentialism, antispeciesism, gender theory, etc.) engaged in intense "conceptual lobbying"[3] are coming into increasing conflict with common sense. For another, a particularly brutal form of stupidity has erupted in the public sphere, thanks to the internet and to social networks that furnish it with a formidable echo chamber.

There's no better example of the current rapprochement between stupidity and Newspeak than the message that was published on Facebook in March 2018 by a militant vegan after a terror attack in the French town of Trèbes in which a butcher was killed:

"So, huh—you're shocked that a murderer would get killed by a terrorist? Not me. I've got zero compassion for him, there's even some justice in it."

Here we find a concentration of everything most characteristic of contemporary Newspeak, transformed into sheer stupidity.

A Shift in the Frame of Reference: When Words Come Apart

What most shocks common sense in this message is, of course, the characterization of the butcher as a "murderer." This term seems simultaneously improper, hyperbolic, insulting, and in the end, stupid. It's of the same order as the word "fags," which a sports commentator recently used off-mike to describe players on a German football team who had insulted a French club.

The stupid things people say are, primarily, a kind of false front, often tinged with exaggeration. The words they use correspond neither to their habitual meaning nor to the referent they're supposed to designate. However, it's different from lying, because the people who say stupid things do not really intend to deceive their audience. They're just venting. Certainly, without the slightest concern for truth; but also without the least pretense of being taken seriously; that is, to be taken at their word. This last point might seem, at first glance, to distinguish between the stupidity of those who use Newspeak from the stupidity of a person for whom, on the contrary, every word matters because it expresses a strong belief. Let's look at what's going on here.

In calling the butcher who was the victim of a terrorist a "murderer," the vegan militant is surely not aware of saying something stupid. Quite the contrary. She uses this term in perfect consciousness that it departs from its ordinary meaning. Through it, she fiercely asserts a lexical readjustment that, in her judgment, renders the language more truthful, and better able to reflect reality. Killing animals, in her eyes, is objectively murder; and therefore, to describe a killer of animals as a murderer is to use the right word, even if the validity of this is not obvious to everyone. Taking a similar approach, you could for example allege that, in the time of slavery, the murder of a slave was not regarded as homicide, either! Seen this way, the apparently outrageous use of the word "murderer" in the butcher incident would merely anticipate a meaning that later would be unanimously accorded. This hypothesis is plausible: in its transformation of the old language, particularly in the meaning of its words, Newspeak in many cases can look like progress. But is that the case here?

Obviously not. First of all, there is the simple fact that, in our day, butchers do not kill animals—that's done in slaughterhouses. Their job is to carve their carcasses into steaks, filets, and so on. Therefore, the descriptor "murderer" lacks exactness, and constitutes a lexical impropriety.

Here we touch on a point that brings the language of ideology and the language of stupidity into close communion: the shift in frame of reference that makes words come unscrewed, if we may put it that way, from their relation to reality,[4] even if we can't quite categorize these improper uses of language as lies. The idiot sports commentator on French TV doesn't really believe that the foes of his favorite team are all homosexual. As for the high-minded militant, it never occurred to her that the butcher she denounced had in all likelihood never slain a single creature. In this sort of discourse, words do not refer to themselves, they become "their own referents." They transmit a kind of delusion, like a fetish whose significance exceeds its true nature.[5]

The Inconsistency of the Signified: Is a Murderer Always a Murderer?

However, this recourse to the referential function of language is not enough to resolve the debate about proper usage of vocabulary; that is, to distinguish the wheat from the chaff, right words from wrong ones. It's necessary to pin down the definitions of the words in question to examine what they signify, because the words serve less to describe the world around us than to help us analyze it and give it meaning with the help of concepts that we can identify.

We could point out to the woman who used the word "murderer" that if the act of killing an animal constituted murder, then the cat who catches and kills a mouse would have to be described as a murderer, as would the whale who exterminates krill, or the cheetah who, for its dinner, disembowels an antelope. Correct word usage demands that the signified possess a stable definition that can be used to designate different referents if they share the same qualities. If, therefore, killing an animal is criminal when a human being does it, it logically follows that the same act is just as criminal if another animal does it. One way or another, our defender of animal rights ought to applaud the idea of the extinction of all carnivores, through the providential "justice" she invokes at the end of a message whose consequences she had not necessarily thought through. Her heedless, unreflective language embodies the principal shared features of Newspeak and stupidity, each as liable as the other to prompt people to spout thoughtless blunders and make occasional gaffes. But that's not all.

Blinkered Words, Humpty Dumpty Style

In a way, words that free themselves from their referents and proper meanings escape the ordinary confines of language. But a word is always a problematic entity: its meaning is open, and can be the object of negotiation between two interlocutors,[6] each of whom attempts in turn to assert (with greater or lesser persuasiveness) its relation to the referent or its conceptual coherence, affirming or denying that it is the right word on a case-by-case basis.

From this point of view, language is a dialectical reality as well as a dialogical one, and only an individual as tyrannical as Humpty Dumpty, in *Through the Looking-Glass*, can declare, in "rather a scornful tone" to boot, that "When *I* use a word ... it means just what I choose it to mean—neither more nor less." That's exactly what idiots and ideologues do. Their words, arbitrarily defined and with no relation to anything but themselves, are not open to the least discussion. This is the ultimate perversion of language, because language belongs to everyone.

Since the idiot, like the ideologue, is unaware of the diversity of reality or of the multiplicity of points of view,[7] his words have blinkers on them. They signify "neither more nor less" than what he or she who uses them imperiously decides, with no more regard for other speakers than for the tradition reflected in the dictionary. If this person (who, let us recall, prides herself on having "zero compassion") decides that the word "murderer" is the best way to define the butcher's trade, well, that's what this word, which has become self-referential because of the inconsistency of its definition, will signify. But such words are no longer truly words; they have become one-way signals whose meaning no longer lends itself to interpretation.

Paradoxically, because they permit no discussion, these signal words become inarguable when they are dictatorially imposed in conversation. They therefore can only be unquestioningly accepted, or challenged . . . which brings its own risks and dangers.

Slogans: The Battle Cries of the Herd[8]

These signal words constitute slogans in an etymological sense (the word "slogan" comes from the Gaelic, designating the battle cry that rallied members of the same clan). They are not used so much to say something that could generally be better expressed another way, as to dignify the group they identify with, formally or informally. (Conversely, those who don't use these terms, or worse, who reject them, exclude themselves from the group in question, making themselves irredeemable enemies of the speaker.) Deriding the German rivals to a French football team as "fags" is a way of affirming one's support of the French team as a patriot, as a man proud of his heterosexuality, etc. In the same manner, the message the militant posted on Facebook simultaneously denotes a desire for complicity, through the familiar tone she takes as she addresses her virtual audience ("So, huh—"), and a desire for distinction, demonstrated by the appeal she makes to iconoclasts by announcing her opposition to majority opinion and consensus ("you're shocked? . . . Not me.").

This apparent critical spirit, this provocativeness—which never departs from what the group she identifies with would approve—is common both to the idiot and to the ideologue. Despite their simplistic rhetoric—or rather, because of it— both groups draw on a know-it-all's sense of superiority. Such feelings account for a large part of linguistic stupidity, as well as for the startling, unshakable success of demagogues. The latter, like the former, frequently resort to sweeping generalizations that are peremptory, assured . . . and for that reason, reassuring. One of the most powerful antidotes to the delirium of ideology is doubt, the intellectual check to stupidity.

The Loss of Common Sense

The current ideological foment, fostered by, among other factors, algorithms and social networks that spawn niche cultures and bring together members of diverse groups, facilitates the spread of jargon that bears increasingly less resemblance to ordinary speech. At the same time, social networks dissolve the boundaries of these groups, giving rise to confusion about what is private or semiprivate and what can be made public; in other words, what can and cannot be publicly said.

After the activist's post (which was shocking to most people) was denounced by other internauts who did not share her vocabulary or her *a priori* ideology, the young woman's first reaction was to protest that "this post was only addressed to [her] friends," and then to appeal to "L214," the animal rights association she identified with. Unfortunately for her, the association soon sent out a communiqué dissociating itself from her statement.

As for the disgraceful remark of our sports commentator; without the ill will of a third party, it would never have been made public, and therefore would not have given rise to the scandal it produced.

These two anecdotes reveal a crisis in public discourse, mined on every side by two forms of linguistic abuse that, while different, are united in one essential thing, the loss of common sense. We are dealing on one side with conceptual idiocy that often has its origins in the humanities, but remains

more or less abstruse and shocking to most people (rape culture, gender issues, state racism, etc.); on the other side, with a
provocative vulgarity that invades the public sphere uninten-
tionally (as in the case of our sports commentator), or inten-
tionally (as manifested, for example, in the tweets of President
Trump or the Vaffanculo Days ["Fuck You" Days] organized
in Italy by the populist Five Star Movement party).

The thinking public struggles to juggle these two forms of
abuse to protect common sense, without which no consensus
in words or discourse is even minimally possible. Public debate is reduced to a clash of slogans, whose opponents don't
debunk them, but simply reject them, denouncing them as
senseless. Given that field studies on the subject of stupidity,
like the one conducted by René Zazzo cited earlier, have
shown that everyone is always a fool in somebody else's esti-
mation, you can guess the sterility of such ideological con-
frontations.

Stupidity being contagious, the worst thing about this state
of affairs is that all of us lose out when common sense disap-
pears. Magistrates punished the militant vegan for her apology
for terrorism; while web surfers expressed outrage at the
sportscaster's obvious (in their opinion) homophobia. It's worth
asking if taking those two troublemakers literally (whose excessive language did not merit it) did not itself demonstrate a
remarkable lack of open-mindedness, by taking seriously something that should have been recognized for what it was: simple
stupidity.

EMOTIONS DON'T (ALWAYS) MAKE US STUPID

⌐⁓⌐

A Conversation with
❯ Antonio Damasio ❮

*Professor of neurology and psychology and director
of the Brain and Creativity Institute at the
University of Southern California, Los Angeles*

Q. Conventional wisdom holds that emotions make us stupid. Is it stupid to think that?

A. That belief is too general to do justice to the complexity of the problem. First, there's a great variety of emotions. Some of them make us incredibly intelligent when they are appropriate to the situation; and others can make us act completely stupidly or dangerously. So we have to distinguish negative emotions like anger, fear, or contempt, for example, from positive emotions, like joy or compassion, which make us better, help us cooperate, and make us act more intelligently. Of course, every emotion can have a downside: if you're too compassionate or too nice, you can be taken advantage of without any benefit to yourself. We can't put all emotions in the same bag. And let's not forget that it's the situation that determines whether our behavior will prove intelligent or stupid.

Emotions and feelings don't arise in isolation: reason is required to judge our actions. This is important from an evolutionary perspective, because in the beginning, our species felt emotions, but our ancestors weren't aware of that. It's only later on that feelings came on the scene; which is to say, a capacity for reflection on our emotions. All of this is capped by reason, based on relevant knowledge and understanding of a given situation. Intelligence in human beings is the capacity to negotiate between emotional reactions on one hand, and between knowledge and reason on the other. The problem isn't emotion alone, or reason alone. Reason alone is a little dry: it can be appropriate in certain situations in our social lives, but not in all of them, far from it.

Q. **You've shown that when patients are cut off from their emotions because of a cerebral lesion, it's very difficult for them to make good decisions. This would seem to mean that in normal situations, reason and emotion are not opposed.**

A. Exactly. There, too, it's a question of negotiation. It's not possible for a human being to operate at full capacity with reason alone, or with the emotions alone. Both are necessary. In a way, reason evolved from emotions that stay in the background, involving us in a situation or leaving us out of it. The idea that you should only rely on emotions, or only rely on reason, to lead your life . . . now that would be truly idiotic!

Q. **Why is it that very intelligent, highly educated people can believe in extremely stupid, even dangerous, things?**

A. We must accept the fact that the immense complexity of the human being provides us with an enormous amount of knowledge, but also with an incredibly broad range of possible reactions. And while psychology and neuroscience are developing general models of human functioning, we shouldn't deduce from this that all of us function the same way. That would be a very big mistake, and a very great danger. Certainly, we're all human, and we all deserve respect, freedom, and kindness. Just the same, we're all extremely different; each of us has our own repertoire of behavior, our own intellectual life, our emotional style, our temperament.

Some of us are very funny and energetic, and wake in the morning singing, while others prefer to sleep in. We need to recognize this almost infinite variety. Also, we don't live alone, but among other humans, amid the culture that has inspired our development. By virtue of this variety, it's altogether possible to believe idiotic things even when we know that they're false in scientific and statistical terms. We're all so different that even speaking of Western culture is debatable. Really, we live in microcultures. French culture, American culture, even that's too general. Of course, you can easily recognize some traits as typically French or American, but they're little more than stereotypes: you also have to reckon with the subdivisions that apply to our social groups, traditions, and behavior norms.

That sounds complicated, but the reality is simply that we can't be reduced to stereotypes. In any case, we shouldn't be.

Q. Your last book, *The Strange Order of Things*, examines the biological roots of culture. Do you think that today, in our global culture, we're living in a golden age of stupidity?

A. Hard to say! In my opinion, yes and no. We don't know everything nowadays, but we know much more than we ever did before. The accumulation of scientific knowledge about biology, for example, on climate, physics, and human diseases like cancer, has never attained this peak before. We've made immense progress. That said, because of the way that information comes to us, especially through digital communication and social networks, we're also living in an age in which we can easily be fooled, and allow ourselves to be influenced by errors or lies. Once again, this means that the answer can't be binary. It depends on who you are and where you are. In hindsight, we know far more now than we did ten years ago, that's inarguable; but we're still subject to streams of disinformation that are being deliberately issued. It's completely contradictory. This age is the best and the worst age for stupidity, rolled into one.

Q. Are the advances in neuroscience sometimes stupid or dangerous?

A. Whatever the case, they interest us very much: we want to know what we're like: how our brain, our mind, and our biology work—which explains why neuroscience is so popular. When a discipline is this fashionable it runs the risk of being abused by bad practitioners. Obviously, there's both good and bad science, but it's not a question of stupidity. And I don't think that neuroscience on the whole is any worse than physics, climatology, or the other sciences.

Interview by Jean-François Marmion.

STUPIDITY AND NARCISSISM[1]

⌐⁓⌐

› Jean Cottraux ‹

Honorary psychiatrist of the hospitals and founding member
of the Academy of Cognitive Therapy of Philadelphia

Two intellectuals, sitting on their duffs,
won't get as far as a brute who walks.

—MICHEL AUDIARD, *TAXI FOR TOBROUK* [*UN TAXI POUR TOBROUK*]

t's hard to define stupidity, and often difficult to perceive it in ourselves and others. Nevertheless, the eminent cognitive psychologist René Zazzo has done research on this subject. Zazzo was a brilliant man who specialized in the study of intelligence, and of self-image, which has considerable bearing on intelligence. He did not hesitate to publish the results of this study, which sparked controversy in academia, his own milieu.

The study involved a hundred doctors, psychiatrists, and psychologists at a big Parisian hospital, and also included twenty members of the Parisian psychiatric community. He gave them a list of 120 names, including their own, asking them which names deserved to be labeled "stupid." Zazzo also put his own name on the list. He doesn't mention his score. . . .

A short list of five names tagged by more than 85 percent of those participating emerged, but only one name was tagged by all of the voters. It was a big boss, a good clinician, whose IQ was at least 120, but who had no sense of humor. He was quite erudite, but he had difficulties connecting with others, little empathy, and a lack of sensitivity that led him to hurt and humiliate people without being aware of it. His logical intelligence was perfect, but he made gaffes because he didn't take others into consideration. In effect, he was trapped in his own narcissistic bubble.

According to this study, therefore, a fool is someone who, lacking emotional intelligence, is blind to his own faults, and who abuses others because of his egocentrism. This description comes close to explaining the narcissistic personality disorder, which I will describe here through its intersection with work, romantic relationships, and social networks.

The Narcissistic Personality Disorder

This disorder is characterized by a general tendency to fantasies and grandiose behavior, accompanied by the need for admiration and a lack of empathy.[2] According to studies, it affects anywhere from 0.8 percent to 6 percent of the general population[3] and is increasingly common in the young generations born after the rise of the internet.[4,5]

A well-conducted study has shown that there are three principal types of narcissistic personality disorder.[6]

1. The malignant and grandiose narcissistic personality
   is manipulative, exploitative, tyrannically deceitful,
   hostile, aggressive, and without empathy. His
   grandiosity does not derive from a need to make up
   for some deficit, but from his sense of entitlement.
   The central disorder of this type of person,

therefore, is their permanent overestimation of themselves. The malignant narcissist resembles the antisocial personality, except for the fact that he's neither impulsive nor risk taking nor irresponsible. He's often adaptable and knows how to retreat when challenged. This makes him even more dangerous to his chosen victims.

2. The unstable narcissistic personality is fragile, depressive, anxious, critical, and envious, has excessively high goals, and can be perfectionist. He masks his feelings of inferiority with grandiosity, which surfaces when he feels threatened.

3. The high-functioning narcissistic personality is grandiose, competitive, exhibitionistic, seductive, and charismatic, on a perpetual quest for power. But on the positive side, he's energetic, intelligent, skilled at relationships, and oriented to self-actualization. This is the narcissism of a number of great directors, artists, and scientists.

These three major disorders should be distinguished from banal contemporary cultural narcissism, which has its origins in the consumer culture that arose in the 1960s, exacerbated by recent developments in technologies of mass communication that have landed us all in the culture of narcissism for three generations.[7]

knowledge that rests on intuition and feeling, a form of stupidity characterized by self-delusion. This means it cannot be challenged, while it strains to resemble a rational, frank, and pertinent concern for truth. From this very broad point of view, it becomes clear that bullshit, fake news, conspiracy theories, and "alternative facts," along with the unintentional "sharing" of them, are contemporary, exacerbated manifestations of good old eternal folly. It's not a big surprise: anyone can see—except, of course, for fools—that post-truth definitely enfolds a prodigious pack of lies.

It remains for us to examine a few of its manifestations and consequences. We have seen that stupidity implies a usurpation of the intellectual domain, but this would not be terribly serious if stupidity did not also extend into the domain of ethics. "The fool," according to the philosopher Pascal Engel, "is guilty of not respecting the truth." His deficit of intellectual virtues translates into a moral vice. Worse still, the man who considers himself a "wit," the bullshitter par excellence, who pretends to respect the values of intelligence and seems to concern himself with the truth and with making sense, in reality only mimics these qualities to gain access to a sphere where he can pass himself off as an intellectual, or just shine a little in society with very little effort. A person who is not a bullshitter, but just isn't all that bright, if you want to put it that way, may well respect the truth and the sort of intelligence that produces it. The bullshitter, the snob, the conceited twit, and the fool have contempt for such simple souls and exploit them, not out of any concern for the truth in itself, but out of self-regard.

The variety of annoying bullshitters is infinite: there's the blowhard who acts like he's expressing new and interesting thoughts or divulging a radical, prodigiously audacious idea; the hypocrite who acts virtuously only so he can tell everyone about it; and, a corollary, the self-righteous moron who expresses moral outrage with the sole purpose of broadcasting his outrage, a very common phenomenon lately, known as "moral grandstanding."[20]

The fool immediately responds to a given assertion or event by feeling and displaying his disapproval, his rejection, his outrage and his anger . . . simply because he has decided that this is what he needs to do, and that it will be useful for him. He will share his reaction with the largest number of people possible, to help him define himself as an individual. This attitude triggers a mechanism of self-polarization, because keeping track of all the possible causes and motives for indignation requires vigilance at all times, producing an escalation of outrage that is aimed at heightening his profile in the competitive arena of stupidity.

Apart from the specific types of annoyance that each brand of bullshitter inflicts on his targets, it must be marked that the overall effect of bullshit, fake news, "alternative facts," and the post-truth world that contains them does not consist, properly speaking, of inciting false beliefs. That was the result, intentional or not, of old-style rumors and propaganda. Today, it has more to do with completely destabilizing our relationship with the truth and eroding faith in the democratic project. To believe in nothing, to not even imagine the possibility that knowledge could be obtained that would come close to establishing a common basis for truth, is probably more pernicious than simply believing in false things, which at least stand the chance of being corrected one day.

All of this amounts to staggering stupidity, which offers almost no grounds for optimism. And yet, we must note that the very existence of post-truth supposes a backdrop of truth, a context in which truth might thrive, if only in the attempt to imitate it. The counterfeit can only cause damage up to a point; beyond a certain threshold, if there's practically nothing but counterfeit money in circulation, it's no longer of any use to anyone. The question that now confronts us is how far stupidity can go, and to what extent it can proliferate through technological platforms that seem to have been conceived to exploit, increase, and broadcast it as far and as fast as possible.

Will this be enough to encourage the younger generations to develop their critical thinking, or to train them to decode information, knowing that the problems they'll face down the line are not the same ones they're facing today? Stupidity, as we've seen, has already adapted to mimic "critical thinking," and even seeks solutions to some of the problems that it itself has created, without, of course, regarding itself as the cause. Is it possible for the epistemological authorities of science, the press, and justice to join this battle by, for instance, proposing greater data transparency, clearer communication, assiduous fact-checking, and laws that discourage and restrict manipulative and malevolent peddlers of misinformation? Probably; but keep in mind that the post-truth world will make mincemeat of each of these initiatives, immediately recycling them through its benighted system that generates erosion of confidence, generalized suspicion, and indifference to facts.

There is still a third option, which would be to beat bullshit at its own game (along with the stupidity that underlies it) by exploring fakery and folly in creative ways. This is the work of satire and fiction, since, after all, a post-truth world implies a post-fiction world. Not to care about truth is not to care if truth is fiction. Perhaps all we need to do to become a little less stupid is to reclaim our taste for the ingenuity of the human mind and to show more intellectual modesty by using our brains to work on behalf of intelligence, not stupidity.

THE
METAMORPHOSES
OF NATIONALIST
FOLLY

> Pierre de Senarclens <

*Honorary professor of international relations at the
University of Lausanne, former executive at UNESCO and
the International Federation of the Red Cross*

Societies need myths. The philosopher Ernst Cassirer attributed the absurdity and contradictions of these imaginary constructions to the "primitive stupidity" of the human being. He rallied around the hypotheses of anthropologists, Bronislaw Malinowski in particular, who interpreted these beliefs as attempts to answer the unsolvable mystery of death. He also saw myths as the expression of collective desires, and did not think societies could get rid of them. He was worried about this: "It's probable that the most important and unnerving aspect of modern political thought is the apparition of a new power: the power of mythical thinking," he wrote in 1945, toward the end of his life, in the United States.[1] Nationalism was part of this mythical thinking, especially since it had undergone disastrous metamorphoses with the emergence of fascist regimes.

In many aspects, this ideology resembles those narratives imbued with magic that the ancient Greeks absorbed in stories "that nursemaids told to distract or frighten children."[2]

Democracy: From Reason to the Passions

The democratic ideal, the inheritance of the Enlightenment, assumed the progress of reason. By this theory, the superstitions and dross of animism would disappear, thanks to improvements in education and the advance of science. Citizens would learn from experience. Deliberations over their circumstances would be based on empirical propositions, paving the way to a choice of the best political options. To this end, they would elect enlightened leaders. Their knowledge and their material conditions would improve, and they would find themselves furnished with the means of securing their freedom and directing the course of their history.

This conviction has proved to be illusory, in part. Societies need some element of the sacred. Reason has proved to be a weak remedy for curbing conflicts of interest, arbitrating between different values, and moderating the power dynamics that constitute the drama of political life. Individuals apply their reason to public life, but also bring everything that animates their psychological reality: their fantasies, their desires, their unconscious impulses, and even their instincts. The influence of ideologies is as bound up with the historic ends they seek as with the emotions they summon and the excesses of violence they justify.

The imperative of national sovereignty, too, was originally imposed as a rational project, tied to citizens' aspirations to autonomy, dignity, and equality. Yet this ideal was particularly charged from an emotional standpoint: it came into being amid a framework of sacred ceremonies analogous to those of religious cults. In this context, several examples may be mentioned: during the French Revolution, the Convention organized a "Feast of Reason" on November 10, 1793, on the square in front of Notre Dame; and during the eruption of fascism in the twentieth century, Mussolini and Hitler organized massive rallies devoted to the cult of those leaders. With the advance of democracy toward the end of the twentieth century, politics became everybody's business, the great theater of individual and collective passions, of intellectuals, political militants, and the masses who invaded the public space with their material demands, their desires, and their fantasies.

The individuals committed to a society's cultural imagination, be it ethnic, religious, or national, may experience all kinds of emotions; but above all, they construct a sense of identity. In embracing nationalist convictions, they appropriate an edifying collective ideal. This inclination is not a problem in itself, but the narcissism that animates it can become a source of pernicious illusions. It enfolds the idea that their nation is heir to a great history, promised an exceptional destiny. This demand for superiority goes hand in hand with the denigration of everything foreign. This is all the more aggressive because it is always affirmed by groups, more or less structured, like crowds, armies, or political parties, that rise under the aegis of unassailable leaders. In fact, nationalism provides a rational, tolerable answer to the needs of individual dignity, but it also plays to other more or less recognized needs and desires: envy, pride, aggression, and the urge to dominate. In exalting the need for glory, honor, physical force, and virility, nationalism appropriates to itself the aristocratic ideas of the Ancien Régime. It offers individuals, particularly the least sound, the resources to appease their feelings of inadequacy and impotence.[3]

The Group Ideal and Its Opposite

Everything that is evoked by narcissism is fragile in nature. This is why the excessive value attributed to a nation is founded on insecurity, as determined either by socioeconomic vulnerability or by causes of a more psychological nature. It implies a shadowy defense of cultural and political borders. Nationalism has an intimate relationship with xenophobia and racism. The foreigner, whose fantasy of harmonious fusion lies at the heart of his demands, symbolizes everything that puts this fantasy at risk. Nationalists arrogate to themselves the right to speak in the name of their national community and to seek to exclude those they suspect of compromising its cohesion. They use their national ideal to denigrate everything that contradicts their political concepts, projecting their need and desire for protection onto providential rulers or onto mystical images of soothing, maternal Nature. The idealized image of the nation unconsciously evokes the maternal universe of infancy, which excludes those who are perceived as seditious outsiders.

This was particularly the case for Jews at the apogee of nationalism, in the last century. With the rise of nationalism in France and Germany in the twentieth century, Jews were perceived as "intruders," undermining the harmony of the national community. "Every society," wrote Georges Devereux, "creates a group ideal," which necessitates the formation of its opposite. The demonization of the Jew permitted national communities to establish fantasy borders for themselves. "It was the counter-ideal of the group," whose essential function was to "magnify the idea of the group while incarnating—as a red flag—everything that the group was not, and which it must, at all costs, avoid becoming."[4]

After World War II, nationalism persisted in the United States, provoking demands for national sovereignty by movements that opposed colonial imperialism. In contrast, nationalism lost its influence in the majority of European countries. The tragedies engendered by fascist regimes had discredited it, in part, while the ideological systems of the superpowers dominated political debate. Apart from this, the protections of the welfare state and consumer society offered other narcissistic gratifications than those associated with the grandeur and honor of the nation, and the armed defense of its interests.

The Return of Magicians

The "sovereignty" that populist movements embrace today, in opposition to globalism, fosters the return of certain nationalist illusions, particularly the one of a homogeneous national population. It also reintroduces rites that emphasize otherness: rallies, anthems, and banners. This nationalism gives rise both to feelings of group identity and to a need for Magicians in Chief. In this context, the migrant is blamed for falling wages, rising unemployment, and social instability, and is also associated with an "invasion" of people of different races, bearers of foreign cultural values who cause the breakdown of a society's traditional solidarity. The migrant is also a symbol of changing times. His outcast status is all the stronger because he's also regarded as a source of malaise, culpable for society's upheavals. Furthermore, pretty much everywhere, religious sects born out of the failures of national integration perpetuate delusional, exclusionary, and hateful visions that are expressed in nationalism.

The public's aspiration to renew the social contract of national sovereignty proceeds from a rational impulse. It's an answer to the challenges and constraints of an underregulated globalism, which is responsible for a great deal of insecurity, vast migratory movements, new social polarization, and unemployment. Confronted with these economic and social realities at a time when new modes of production and interdependency are emerging, administrations are executing their responsibilities for political integration poorly and struggling to come up with technocratic solutions and paths to reform. These failures are accompanied by the erosion of broad ideological systems with utopian visions, and also with the weakening of traditional measures of socialization, contributing to the impoverishment of democratic deliberation. They prompt some individuals to seek imaginary communities characterized by extraordinary representations of nationhood, ethnicity, and religion, illusions that foster political and social alienation. They incline them to seek the aid of a civil authority, a group endowed with fantastical powers that would be capable of bringing them the protection they crave.

Populism Recruits in Every Sphere

Economic distress does not entirely explain populism, as those who support it do not all belong to materially disadvantaged spheres, especially in the United States. Their vulnerability can also have a psychological character. Voters who support populist leaders whose rhetoric is charged with violence and chants base their choice on identity. Let's consider the case of Donald Trump. During his electoral campaign, his lack of civility was an important aspect of his political success. He did not hide any of his personal failings. He advertised his immaturity, his narcissistic fragility, acting as if he'd never grown up, as if he'd never acquired a true moral conscience. His lies, exhibitionism, incoherence, and bad-boy behavior seduced the public. A large number of Americans, whatever their social status, recognized themselves in his rudeness, his outlandish behavior, his simplistic ideas, his Manichean positions, his conspiracy theories, his racism, and his exaltation of the grandeur of the United States.

Populist parties recruit primarily among those who lack much academic background or professional education—people who are not equipped to fully evaluate the consequences of the options they're choosing. The speeches of these parties rely on the language of polemics, using a narrow range of words and vulgar expressions. They flatter people who have trouble conceiving figurative ideas, or recognizing nuance, or meeting complex challenges fraught with contradictions. These voters have no patience for complicated economic questions and no taste for political debates. Carried away by their rage at the elites, they support programs that conflict with their own interests, as demonstrated by their stance against the liberalization of trade, work, debt, and monetary policy. In abusing the procedures of the democratic process, they paradoxically undermine the legitimacy of the national project.

So, are they stupid? That notion does not belong to the language of social science. If political stupidity were only a question of education, we would know it. Populism mobilizes individuals whose judgment is clouded by emotions and whose passions and personal failures can obscure their cognitive capacities. These seductive magical nostrums and this state of mind contaminate every sphere. That said, the political opinions of the intelligentsia are not infallible. In France, as elsewhere in Europe, fanatical political ideologies, from nationalism and fascism to Stalinism and Maoism, as well as Trotskyism and other bizarre offshoots, often have been supported by people whose cultural refinement is indisputable.[5]

Blame goes here to the evolution of liberal societies, to the dispossession of the individual in the market economy, and to the culture of narcissism that favors these trends. Even if the market economy doesn't benefit as many people as it ought to, it's hard to escape the illusions of consumerism.

It's no coincidence that Donald Trump, Silvio Berlusconi, and Beppe Grillo have played an important role in telereality and the world of spectacle, a cultural stew of myths and magic words. Their made-up world is presented as if it were real, and mobilizes the sphere of individual and collective fantasies. While provoking all sorts of antisocial impulses, it also gives rise to frustrations linked to the hedonistic desires it excites. The growing heterogeneity of socialization processes, tied to the expansion of familial structures and the erosion of institutional and normative frameworks like civic solidarity, has no real connection to the rise in power of the brand of incivility that favors populism. Faced with these dramatic social shifts, the safeguarding of democracy, like the fight against the coarsening of society, hinges on the defense of principles, frameworks, and institutional equilibrium necessary to the protection of the rule of law. It also requires the active pursuit of a politics whose goal is social justice.

HOW CAN WE FIGHT
COLLECTIVE ERROR?

> Claudie Bert <

Science journalist specializing in the humanities

n his first book, published in 2002, Christian Morel, a former human resources executive turned sociologist, gives several examples of what he calls "absurd decisions."[1] In one example, two oil tankers follow nearly parallel routes, but one of them changes course, blocking the path of the other, which then cannot avoid colliding with it; in another, a plane is beginning the landing process when the pilot, under the impression that the landing gear has not come down, continues circling to give the cabin crew time to prepare the passengers for a rough landing—and the plane crashes for lack of fuel.

Too Much Hierarchy Kills

The author also identifies "meta-rules," intended to increase the reliability of decisions that are being progressively imposed, or that are in the process of being imposed, in these different risk zones. The most interesting aspect of these meta-rules is that they are often counterintuitive. For instance, we all have an image of a commander or a pilot as "the man in charge." If anyone were to ask us: "What should we do in an emergency?" we would doubtless respond, "Definitely, this man must be obeyed in an emergency, no question!" Well, actually, no. Strict obedience to hierarchy is a risk factor, as established in the case of Korean Air. During the 1990s, that airline fell victim to a series of fatal accidents that investigations attributed to one principal factor: the excessively hierarchical cockpit culture. The pilot had crashed because of his disregard for his subordinates; neither the copilot nor the mechanic had dared correct a pilot error, etc.

At the beginning of the 2000s, Korean Air's new director profited from the findings of these investigations by implementing a series of practices that were totally contrary both to past procedures and to the country's cultural traditions. Under the new rules, the hierarchy had to be open to communication; promotion would depend on merit, not seniority; all pilots would be educated in human factors; and the policy of nonsanction of errors would be implemented. Result: today the company is among the safest in the world. This policy of nonsanction of errors also runs counter to common opinion. As soon as an accident happens, the same cry goes out everywhere: "Whose fault was it?" But the Federal Aviation Administration, which controls aviation in the United States, including airlines like Korean Air and Air France, calls on flight personnel to report every error in detail—anonymously. In the medical establishment, various health procedures have been adopted to report hospital errors in the same manner. This way the mistakes can be better understood and more easily avoided.

Unanimity? Mistrust!

Another piece of evidence that flouts common sense concerns the decisions made by a group. If the decision is unanimous, surely it must be right? Again, no. In high-risk settings, experience has shown that "false consensus" should be feared: members of a group often keep quiet because they're afraid of contradicting the boss, or because they think they're in the minority, and so on.

This has led to the adoption of procedures that test supposed consensus: like the obligation for each member of a group to offer his personal opinion; and the systematic inclusion of a devil's advocate charged with defending the minority opinion. The meta-rules cited here concern multiple human behaviors. So it's not shocking to discover that there's a trend for the creation of new education programs, on top of technical training, that take human factors into account in the professional education of pilots, surgeons, or high-altitude mountain guides. The new programs take theoretical and practical group interactions into account to identify factors that influence decisions. A recent study, also cited by Christian Morel, illustrates the value of this kind of education. When seventy-four surgical centers attached to the Veterans Health Administration in the United States adopted this training, surgical mortality rates dropped 18 percent, compared to a decrease of 7 percent in the thirty-four centers that did not adopt it.

As an aside to readers who, not living in a risk zone, don't feel involved: here's an example from everyday life that Morel gave in his first book. A couple is entertaining their married children at their home in Texas. It's 104 degrees in the shade. They're all sipping cool drinks on the deck when the father cries out, "Why don't we go get something to eat in Abilene?" (the "neighboring" town by American standards, a hundred miles round trip). All of them accept. Four hours later, they return and collapse on the deck, exhausted by the heat and depressed by their awful lunch; and they discover that none of them had wanted to go to Abilene, but each of them had thought the other three wanted to! If only they had applied the meta-rule of mistrust of apparent consensus. . . .

WE ALL CONSUME LIKE FOOLS

A Conversation with
› Dan Ariely ‹

Professor of psychology and behavioral
economics at Duke University

Q. How would you define behavioral economics?

A. Before you can answer that question, you first have to explain what "standard economics" is, which is a useful comparison of what behavioral economics is and is not. Standard economics is built around simple questions. For example, what kind of choices people should make in consumption or investment to get the maximum benefit from their decisions. This approach led to the formulation of the rational actor theory, whether that's a consumer or a producer; and departing from that premise, it deduces political conclusions on how the economy should be run: which are the best institutions and decisions to allocate resources to.

Behavioral economics doesn't take off from this point of view. It tries to describe how people behave in real-life situations. Its goal is not to define an ideal of rationality, but to analyze how people actually act. To do that, this field has developed experiments on the way people arbitrate between several choices when confronted with an economic decision.

For example, let's start with a simple question: why are

there obese people? The perspective of standard economics would lead us to say that these people are informed consumers, so they're eating what they want to eat, after having calculated the advantages and the costs. And if they eat too much and become obese, that's their choice.

But according to behavioral economics, people become obese for all kinds of other reasons. Many of them would like to eat less and to control their weight better, but when they're in front of their plates, they have a hard time holding back. A lot of them try to lose weight, but they often crack. They're subject to temptations that they have a hard time controlling; they make wrong evaluations of their future activities, like going on a diet. And that's the fundamental difference between standard economics and behavioral economics.

Q. What are the principal influences that behavioral economists have studied?

A. First of all, emotions play an essential role in our buying behavior. Most of our actions are guided by emotion, not reason. If you have the disagreeable experience of finding yourself face-to-face with a tiger, your first reaction will be to flee, not to deliberate over the best action to take. Most of the time, that's how people proceed in daily life.

An emotion like fear is a good counselor: it pushes us to confront a danger. But emotions push us to give in to the stimuli that we're presented with. Most consumer products are conceived to elicit emotional reactions in us. For example, Dunkin' Donuts is devised and presented to inspire sugar and cream cravings. Shop windows display products in the most attractive way possible to provoke temptation in the consumer. That's why, at the supermarket, we often buy more things than we'd meant to at first: our cravings have been stimulated by the presentation of attractive products, thrust before our eyes, in arm's reach.

Faced with these temptations, we of course do have a capacity for self-control. But self-control itself is limited because it's subject to psychological mechanisms that have been well studied by behavioral economics.

Imagine that you give a chocolate lover this option: Would you rather be given half a box of chocolates now, or a full box next week? Even though it's a gift, it's in the interest of the person to wait until the next week. But in reality, most of the time, attracted to the chocolates, the person will prefer to sacrifice her long-term interest to satisfy her immediate desire.

We're constantly subjected to dilemmas like this one in daily life. Take the student who puts off his homework and goes to the movies because he's tempted by a film. His choice of staying in to work or giving in to his temptation is skewed. If he chooses to stay at home, the cost is immediate and the anticipated benefit (a better chance of doing well in his exams) is hypothetical and long-term. On the other hand, if he goes to the movies, the benefit is immediate and the cost of his decision is postponed to the distant future.

That's why we often make immediate decisions that go

against what we'd like to do in the long term. Procrastinators, who always put off until later what they should do at once, know this problem very well.

Q. Is there a way to master the emotions to manage your consumption better?

A. There's no one, sole, simple solution to help people "control" their consumption. But you can find personal tricks to help you make better choices. A few years back, I got a very serious illness that put my life at risk. The doctors gave me a treatment that was really hard to take: the medicine gave me unbearable nausea for hours. A lot of sick people would rather skip certain doses, or even abandon the treatment in spite of the danger. So I invented something to help me get through the ordeal. Each time I had to take my terrible injection, I allowed myself to see a video (one I love). That way, not only was the sickness less horrible to endure, but I'd mentally associated the medicine with a reward instead of a torment. When I knew I was going to have to take the medicine, instead of thinking about distressing pain, I thought about my reward. And it worked! When I finished the treatment, my doctor was surprised: I was the only one of his patients who'd completed the whole course of treatment.

That's one way to trick yourself and overcome your own weaknesses. When you try to control your consumption behavior, it can be useful to invent techniques of this type. But you can also use technologies that spur consumers to control their consumption. It's been shown that Americans significantly lower their electricity consumption in their homes if the electricity company gives them a little glowing lightbulb that turns red when too many electrical appliances are on and consumption has passed a certain threshold.

Finally, there are also political measures that encourage or dissuade consumers or producers from consuming or making certain products rather than others, penalizing products that cause pollution, favoring ethically responsible products, and encouraging people to economize or to limit the debt of their households. Controlled personal choices and public incentives can promote behavioral economics, as reflected by consumption habits.

Interview by Jean-François Dortier.

THE PARADOXES OF ABUNDANCE

Here's an astonishing marketing experiment. Six kinds of jam are presented to consumers on a display table. At the end of the day, they count the number of pots that

were sold. The next day, they put out twenty-four kinds of jam. They compare the sales figures and . . . surprise, sales are higher when there are six types of jam than when there are twenty-four! Moral: Abundance of choice inhibits purchasing.

This experiment was conducted with appropriate controls by Sheena Iyengar, a professor at Columbia University and the author of *The Art of Choosing*. The book puts forth a paradox of our consumer society: the uneasiness provoked by abundance of choice.

When faced with too many options, the consumer is effectively paralyzed. This is an experience anyone might recognize. Back in the age of public television, when there were only three available channels, the television viewer chose his programs quickly. Today, remote control in hand, he can zap for fifteen minutes through the hundreds of channels that are available to him. The excessive range of possibilities reinforces indecision and even provokes a certain feeling of dissatisfaction: the feeling that you haven't found the ideal program.

TOO MUCH CHOICE HARMS CHOICE

It's often said that too much information kills information. Internet users know that the immensity of available resources on the web sometimes confuses the searcher who's looking up a clear, simple fact. The more you refine the question, the more new paths pop up; notions that you thought you understood become more complex, the data accumulates, and you run the risk of suffocating in an avalanche of facts. That's the paradox of the culture of abundance.

In other times, food was a rare commodity and many people suffered from hunger. Today we must learn to restrain ourselves in the face of the abundant and varied gustatory temptations that present themselves to us. The same is true of information: millions of sites are a click away, thousands of television channels can be accessed by the remote control, thousands of books can be found in libraries and bookstores.

In the area of marketing, abundance also harms decision making. In *The Paradox of Choice: Why More Is Less—How the Culture of Abundance Robs Us of Satisfaction*, the sociologist Barry Schwartz addressed the phenomenon of mental overload. In cultures of abundance—of food, information, entertainment—our problem is not to find resources, but to narrow them down. *J.-F. D.*

THE HUMAN:
THE ANIMAL THAT
DARES ALL

> Laurent Bègue <

*Member of the Institut Universitaire de France and director
of the Maison des Sciences de l'Homme-Alpes*

We love cows, but we eat them all the same.

—ALAIN SOUCHON, "SANS QUEUE NI TÊTE"
["NEITHER HEAD NOR TAILS"]

Salvos of the royal cannon sounded in the crowded forecourt of the Palace of Versailles. It was exactly 1:00 p.m., and on this nineteenth of September 1783, in front of Louis XVI and his family, a duck, a rooster, and a sheep placidly entered the annals of aerospace. Having taken up residence in the wicker basket attached to the hot-air balloon of the brothers Montgolfier, the barnyard denizens soon rose 650 yards up in the air and traveled several miles, to the cheers of the amazed onlookers. Despite the misfortune of the rupture of the balloon, which would abridge their historic flight, the three woolly and feathered heroes landed in the Bois de Vaucresson. They were royally rewarded by the Dauphin, who opened the doors of his menagerie to them. Only a few weeks after the exploit of the involuntary aeronauts, humans would take to the air, at less risk.

Ever since then, animals both aquatic and terrestrial (quail, jellyfish, cats, dogs, monkeys, salamanders) have been propelled by the dozens into the stratosphere, and not always with the good fortune of their three ancestors. Even now, in the twenty-first century, humanity decimates countless animals, not only to conduct scientific experiments, but for industrial production and for food. Nearly 100 million of them are used in laboratories around the world every year,[1] 70 billion birds and mammals are slaughtered for food, and a trillion fish are caught. To make such levels of production possible, we have not only developed sophisticated scientific protocols and methods of animal husbandry, we have also put in place psychological mechanisms that permit us to ignore or to legitimize the harms of this exploitation.

If the troubles that *Homo sapiens* inflicts on other species did not have unfavorable consequences for human existence itself, we could speak only of insensitivity or cruelty and not address the facetious subject raised by this article's title. Alas, through its generalized exploitation of animals, humanity takes the risk of embarking on its own version of the hot-air balloon ride with the damaged balloon: traveling in hazardous conditions. Some authors today are publishing works for the general public with strident titles about ecological disaster and the barbarousness of industrial farming (*Farmageddon*) or denouncing overfishing (*Aquacalypse*), but in spite of these warnings, we are turning a deaf ear. That is because the species we belong to possesses the dangerous privilege of being endowed with psychological tools that permit us the spectacular folly of prospering through a senseless relationship with other animals.

Henri IV, the king who promised "a chicken in every pot on Sundays," was fortunate to have a famous finance minister, Sully, who liked to proclaim that "pasture and labor are the two teats of France." Expanding upon this rural idyll, we will propose here that France has three teats when it comes to the human folly of its rapport with animals: logical incoherence, ignorance, and rationalization.

The Teat of Illogic

In his book on carnivory, *L'Imposture Intellectuelle des Carnivores*[2] [*The Intellectual Imposture of Carnivores*], Thomas Lepeltier shares his disingenuous perplexity at our illogic: "If you grind up kittens in a blender, castrate a dog without anesthesia, or shut up a horse for its entire life in a minuscule enclosure where daylight does not penetrate, you will be pursued by the law for cruelty to animals. You might get sentenced to two years in prison. So why do public authorities permit people to grind up living male chicks, shut up chickens all their lives in minuscule cages, and slit the throats of millions of rabbits, lambs, pigs . . . ?" The law preserves this illogic and perpetuates it, under the understanding that, although "animals are living, sentient creatures," according to the "laws that protect them, animals are subject to the regulations that affect property" (Article 515-14 of the French Civil Code). Take the case of the rabbit: today it is one of the most common house pets in France, but it's also the mammal that is most frequently consumed. If we do not meet our obligation to feed a pet rabbit, care for it, and provide it with living conditions appropriate to its needs, we are at great risk of breaking the law, since "the fact of committing an abuse of a serious or sexual nature against a pet or other domesticated animal, or an animal kept in captivity, in public or not, is

punishable by two years in prison and a fine of 30,000 euros"
(Article 521-1 of the French Penal Code). And yet, the law au-
thorizes the practice of rabbit battery farming in conditions of
unmitigated confinement.

But a rationale of another order hides behind this seeming
illogic. In effect, the value of an animal falls on a sliding scale,
determined by the animal's instrumental utility or its emotional associations, or upon the justifications that humans
make concerning the species in question. This is also the case
with defenders of animal rights. According to the observations
of one veterinarian, the activists who fight against animal testing act more often against laboratories or researchers that use
primates or dogs than those that use mice or rats. Almost two-
thirds of people who believe that one of the priorities of the
animal rights movement should be the abolition of the use of
their skins in clothing manufacture admit to wearing leather
clothes or shoes. This anthropocentrism, which bases an animal's value on human associations, is the key to the hierarchy
that we impose on different animals.

The Teat of Ignorance

For anyone who has a relationship with animals, ignorance is
the most consoling comfort. Recently, the circus performer
André-Joseph Bouglione, who has resolved to stop using animals in his shows completely, confessed that "the slight sway-
ing the elephants made when they were at rest used to make

me feel like they were relaxed . . . but what I'd thought was a sign of relaxation turned out in fact to be linked to confinement."[3] Lack of awareness of the cognitive, perceptive, and sensory capacities of animals has facilitated their subjection for centuries, as suggested by Descartes' notion of the "animal machine," described in his *Discourse on Method* (which holds that animals are machines incapable of thinking), perhaps to justify vivisection, a practice he himself conducted in the name of science. "It cries out, but it does not feel," swore Malebranche, as he beat his dog. But let's not denounce our old philosophers; stupidity exists in every age. In June 2017, *The Washington Post* published an online poll of a representative sample of Americans. Seven percent of the respondents (more than 16 million people) believed that chocolate milk came from brown cows. From bad to worse, a poll by the U.S. Department of Agriculture revealed that one adult in five did not know which animal hamburger meat comes from. Two researchers from the University of California, Davis, Alexander Hess and Cary Trexler, interviewed eleven- and twelve-year-old children and found that 40 percent of them didn't know that the meat in hamburgers comes from cows, and only 30 percent knew that cheese was made from milk. Alimentary ignorance is similarly striking on this side of the Atlantic: a French poll of eight- to twelve-year-olds showed that 40 percent did not know where products like ham came from, and two-thirds could not identify the origin of steak. Beyond that, an elevated percentage of children declared that fish had no bones. What might be the proportion of the little darlings who imagine that the mammary glands of cows spontaneously produce milk when there's no calf to feed? All bets are open.

Age-old human ignorance of animal cognition has favored the relationship of domination, which remains hard to correct despite progress in cognitive ethology and neuroscience. Nevertheless, experts today believe that "non-human animals have the neuroanatomical, neurochemical, and neurophysiological substrates of conscious states along with the capacity to exhibit intentional behaviors" (*Cambridge Declaration on Consciousness*, 2012), and there's no shortage of works that demonstrate that dumb animals aren't so dumb, after all.[4,5] But the simple diffusion of knowledge is not enough to curb the extravagances of reason. More and more groups involved with monetizing livestock production are devising ingenious ways to spread a bucolic, idyllic image of smiling cows, and chickens that yearn to land on the dinner table. As the philosopher Florence Burgat[6] has observed, the disincarnation of meat and the erasure of the animal involved in its production contribute to an elaborate euphemization of the realities of raising livestock and the slaughter that the industry entails. The philosopher Martin Gibert[7] writes that in 2013, the magazine *Paysan Breton Hebdo* [*Breton Rural Weekly*] prudently informed farmers, "You must 'de-animalize' the product, that is, to sever the connection it may have with the animal, and place much more emphasis on the end product." Applying the same dissembling optics, a magazine for professionals in the meat business cited by Scott Plous of Wesleyan University noted that "to remind a consumer that the rack of lamb he's just bought is part of the anatomy of one of those cute little creatures you see gamboling on hillsides in springtime is probably the surest way to turn him into a vegetarian."

Another form of ignorance also deserves mention. It concerns consumers' systematic underreporting of the quantity of meat they eat. For example, several polls indicate that between 60 percent and 90 percent of those who defined themselves as vegetarians had consumed meat in the days preceding the poll. Most studies on vegetarianism reveal that no less than two-thirds of those who call themselves vegetarians occasionally consume chicken, and 80 percent eat fish! And if you tell participants that they will be shown a news report on animal suffering, they will automatically, unconsciously reduce the amount of meat they report consuming. Sometimes, to diminish animal suffering, some consumers stop buying red meat . . . but increase their consumption of poultry, which increases the number of animals consumed and therefore of animals that have truly suffered. (To obtain the equivalent of the meat provided by one solitary cow, 221 chickens must die.)

For those who've truly opted for a meatless diet, it doesn't stop there. Although sausages advertised as "meatless" may taste just as good as sausages made from the flesh of animals, when participants were asked to fill out a questionnaire evaluating a vegetarian sausage they were given to eat, they judged it tastier when they were told it contained meat. Another study showed that people who were given a nutrition bar to consume deemed it less delicious when they were led to believe that it contained soy.

The Teat of Rationalization

Joined to ordinary ignorance is something you could call motivated ignorance. To avert the discomfort of a crisis of conscience over the discrepancy between the behavior of meat consumption and our awareness of the fate of the animals consumed (which might induce us to refrain from eating meat), we modify our awareness through a process explained by the theory of cognitive dissonance. For example, one study demonstrated that the mental capacity we attribute to a range of animals is straightforwardly correlated to their edibility. Cows and pigs are perceived as having a less rich inner life than cats, lions, or antelopes. In another study, participants were asked to rate the mental capacities of a sheep after being informed either that the ovine was going to change its pasture, or that it would be on the menu for an upcoming meal. In the latter case, its mental capacities were underplayed. In a third study (which made it blindingly obvious that human beings think with their taste buds), the participants were briefly introduced to a mammal that is found in New Guinea, Bennett's tree-kangaroo. Next, different facts were presented. In one case, it was explained that the inhabitants of New Guinea eat the animal's meat; in the other, no mention at all was made of the consumption of the animal. Participants were then asked to estimate how much pain this type of kangaroo would suffer if it were injured, and if moral criteria ought to be applied to its treatment. The results indicated that the simple fact of assigning this animal to the edible meat category was enough to modify the sensory traits imputed to it. These perceived capacities, in turn, determined the participants' moral concerns regarding the animal.

Over and over you see this kind of intellectual magic trick that permits us to justify the consumption of meat through reductive conclusions, like Aristotle's statement:[8] "Plants exist for the good of animals, and wild beasts for the good of man"; or through lack of empathy, as in Saint Augustine's statement: "We see . . . that death is painful for animals, but man despises that in the beast"; or through the euphemistic myth of the animal's "consent" to its slaughter (by which it offers us its meat in exchange for our "kind" care); or through the denial of animal suffering ("Animals suffer less if they're conscious when their throats are cut than if they're slaughtered after they've been stunned"); or through the invocation of lofty goals, buttressed by research (like "feeding humanity," or the "argument of the child with cancer to justify scientific research on animals aimed at developing treatments"); or even the declaration that survival depends upon it ("If Man is condemned to vegetarianism, he will not survive"); or the invocation of alimentary aporia (the argument that the carrot "screams" when it's uprooted) and the demonization of vegetarianism (which is accused of misanthropy, and compared with Nazism) . . . and so on.

Human beings have dared all when it comes to animals. We're even known for this, as the screenwriter Michel Audiard has observed—"Idiots dare everything!" But we pay no price for it. One member of our species who is far from an idiot, the philosopher Michel Onfray, recently claimed, "If I thought about it, I'd be a vegetarian." This vow is not challenged by science: ample proof exists that people who eat vegetables are not pea-brained. Better yet, according to an article in the *British Medical Journal*, children whose IQs are higher than average at the age of ten are more likely to adopt a meatless diet as adults, independently of their social class, level of education, and earning power. Nor does emotional intelligence appear to be in short supply among people who refrain from sticking their forks into other creatures—quite the opposite, if you believe the research.

In conclusion, while some hold that meat was crucial to the development of our ancestors' brains, it may be that these days the situation is different.

In this orb suspended in space that we call Earth, something is not right with the turn animals have taken. The growing knowledge of our joint fate, the profusion of risks to public health, and the many portents of ecological disaster call upon us to act more wisely.

MORE MEAT THAN REASON

In France, 99 percent of rabbits, 95 percent of pigs, 82 percent of broiling hens, and 70 percent of laying hens are raised through factory farming. In numerous cases, the living conditions and conditions of slaughter are unacceptable (for example, according to the French slaughterhouse workers' organization OABA, more than half the animals are still conscious when their throats are cut). However, not even taking into account the grinding up of chicks, the force-feeding of geese, and the systematic mutilation of piglets and cows, reasons to question factory farming abound. On the health level, the role of meat in cardiovascular disease and obesity is well established, and its status as a "probable human carcinogen" has been certified by the World Health Organization. In a report on their findings in the journal *PNAS* (*Proceedings of the National Academy of Sciences of the United States of America*), researchers at Oxford University calculated that if humanity opted for a vegetable-based diet, the mortality rate would drop somewhere between 6 percent and 10 percent.

Another irrationality: meat production causes the widescale waste of resources. Twenty-five pounds of vegetables are required to produce one pound of beef (five pounds for chicken, and ten pounds for pork). The FAO (the Organization for Food and Agriculture of the United Nations) estimates that four to eleven calories of vegetables are required to produce a single calorie of meat. The unsustainability of the use of agricultural resources for meat production—a veritable protein factory in reverse—was recently brought to light in another *PNAS* publication. Their findings show that if the vegetables used in the production of beef, pork, dairy products, poultry, and eggs were substituted with vegan production intended for human consumption, each acre would yield from two to twenty times more protein. Based solely on American agricultural data, the authors estimate that this would make it possible to feed an additional 350 million people.

Factory farming also exacts a heavy cost on the environment. It is a principal cause of deforestation, and contributes more than any other human activity to greenhouse gases (14.5 percent of total emissions, as opposed to 13 percent from transportation, according to the FAO). David Robinson, author of *Meatonomics*, writes that "raising animal protein takes up to one hundred times more water, eleven times more fossil fuels, and five times more land" than growing vegetable proteins. (See also Fabrice Nicolino, *Bidoche: L'Industrie de la Viande Menace le Monde* [*A Pound of Flesh: The Meat Industry Threatens the World*].)

Finally, factory farming is regarded as a factor that fosters the development and spread of epidemics. In certain countries, it also threatens the health of the populace, which, by consuming animals who've been fed drugs that ward off infections caused by the confined conditions of industrial farming, contributes to the decline in effectiveness of antibiotics. *L. B.*

WHAT CAN BE DONE ABOUT ASSHOLES?

> Emmanuelle Piquet <

Psychotherapist and founder of the
Chagrin Scolaire centers

he term "asshole" must be defined right off the bat, because you can't fight an enemy you can't name.

You can feel the red-faced fury evoked by the phrase "What a complete asshole!" as opposed to its cousin, "What an idiot!" which has a more affectionate ring, though it also must be inscribed in the registry of insults. The same is true of "moron," and "fool," although, in the thrall of an especially melancholy bout of depression, staring into the mirror, you may prefer "fat fool" to "total loser" or "fucking idiot."[1]

Because the asshole frequently inspires immediate and violent hatred. This is because he considers himself above the rules, social codes, and other people. Objectively, he is often wrong. But the kind of violence that he evinces when he announces (explicitly or implicitly) his immense feeling of superiority to the rest of the world produces a vehement and irrepressible rage in the people around him, or sometimes a paralyzed stupor. In either case, the asshole is satisfied: whether his victims nearly suffocate in the attempt to stifle their fruitless urge to set him on fire, or whether they maintain a stunned silence, the asshole retains his power. When confronted by someone who's more of an asshole than he is, he will hypocriti-cally rein himself in, but with those he judges weaker, he will continue his reign. That means there's every reason in the world for the asshole to keep on being an asshole. Given that he often wins these showdowns, there's no reason to expect him to stop of his own free will.

So it's up to those who suffer from his assholery to fix the problem.

Because, unfortunately, the actions of assholes can leave indelible scars on the psyches of those who are less obnoxious than they are, especially the ones who don't succeed in chang-ing the dynamics of the encounters they endure. But if they *do* manage to change the dynamics, here's the good news: the ass-hole can be stopped in his tracks. If his popularity, influence, or feeling of omnipotence decline, when formerly they had been exceptionally strong, he will see that it's not to his advan-tage to act like a jerk.

Let's take a few examples from the adolescent world, as it's crucial to impede the progress of assholes from tenderest youth.

The Bully

Known for the fear they elicit among their peers, which whets their desire to exercise their exhilarating power, the grade school or high school bully unfailingly chooses a scapegoat who fears his violence and is intimidated by the social domi-

of the pen. I heard the slogan "Down with capitalism": that means nothing! Absolutely nothing. First you have to define the words, which is very complicated, because nobody has the same definition of the word "capitalism." You can cite a thousand examples of this kind, and not just from the present. But these watchwords are transmitted at such speed now, through all the little apparatuses that fill our pockets, that that, yes *that*, has changed. You must always reflect on what is behind the words we hear, behind the things we see.

Q. **Are evil and stupidity related?**

A. Definitely. But fools can be very kind and good. Hitlerian, systemic evil is categorically stupid. It is limited, it knows that one day it will be destroyed by an evil perhaps even graver than itself. To attempt to dominate the world, to exclude and exterminate part of the population and impose a thousand-year Third Reich, that's completely idiotic. That's truly stupidity in action. The tragedy is that the most civilized people on the planet can let themselves be intoxicated by such enormous stupidity. One must always be on guard, that's all. And not just let yourself bang on, for example, when you answer questions on the telephone.

Interview by Jean-François Marmion.

MAKING PEACE WITH YOUR STUPIDITY

› Stacey Callahan ‹

Professor of clinical psychology and psychopathology at the University of Toulouse 2-Jean Jaurès, and researcher at the Center for Studies and Research in Psychopathology and Psychology of Health (CERPPS)

Against stupidity, the gods themselves contend in vain.

—FRIEDRICH SCHILLER

Stupidity is inevitable, because we are human. Our stupid actions are of our own creation—as are our reactions to them.

Synonyms for the word "stupidity" abound: folly, silliness, idiocy, clumsiness, obtuseness.... However, they have a common denominator: the inherent element of mistake. Even the most absurd inanity (a farce, for example), when imposed on others, and not received happily by them, is recognized as a mistake. If the expected humorous effect doesn't come off, it's a shame; the action ends up just looking dumb. But it's rare that stupid actions are knowingly committed.

In Search of Unconditional Self-Acceptance

Two things are infinite: the universe and human stupidity; and I'm not sure about the universe! –Attributed to Albert Einstein

How can we accept who we are, given our imperfections, our limitations, and obviously, our stupidity? In psychology, acceptance is a very fashionable concept. For example, there's mindfulness meditation, in which the individual is asked to reflect on his life quite straightforwardly, without judgment. There's also Acceptance and Commitment (ACT), in which the therapist guides the patient on a course of acceptance of the factors that cause him problems (with himself or with others in his environment) and helps him adopt various strategies to acquire optimal psychological flexibility.

In psychology, the concept of unconditional self-acceptance was mainly advanced by the late American psychologist Albert Ellis through the elaboration of his rational emotive behavior therapy (REBT), a precursor to cognitive therapies.[1] He was inspired by the Stoic philosophers (Epictetus, Seneca), who recommended an attitude of general acceptance to promote happiness. His clinical observations showed him that the human being possesses a tendency, both innate and buttressed by education (parental and other), to accept himself—as long as certain conditions are met, most of them associated with performance or with actions undertaken by the individual. Because our self-acceptance depends on our fulfillment of these conditions, our identity is constructed entirely around our actions. Yet a human being is much more than the sum of his actions: "to do" does not in any circumstance mean "to be." Albert Ellis demonstrated that all humans have qualities and flaws (which are sometimes difficult to differentiate), and the actions and traits of an individual can't give a satisfactory account of his "being." A human being is neither "good" nor "bad"; he simply *is*.[2]

Departing from this premise, Ellis proposes the possibility of accepting oneself in an unconditional way, separating the being from his actions. The actions of an individual can be a source of validation, of course, but should not extend to represent the worth of the individual himself. Ellis calls this notion "unconditional self-acceptance" (USA).

Toward Self-Compassion

The difference between genius and stupidity is that genius has its limits. –ATTRIBUTED TO ALBERT EINSTEIN

Unconditional self-acceptance is based on the worth a person feels for his being, not letting his actions define his identity. Under these conditions, doing something stupid doesn't mean you're a fool. It relates to lived experience, not to identity. Even if we accept the idea that our actions don't define us as a person, the experience of doing something stupid feels uncomfortable. Yet the memory of the most innocuous of our stupid actions fades quickly; at worst, we feel a slight embarrassment after a certain amount of time has elapsed. At best, we can look back and laugh about it.

To optimize this process, it's useful to adopt an attitude of compassion toward ourselves, or self-compassion.[3] While we are more or less inclined to express compassion toward others, self-compassion, like unconditional self-acceptance, is a little harder, because of the lack of real models for it in our education.

Kristin Neff, who teaches psychology of education at the University of Texas at Austin, has identified three important components of self-compassion.[4] The first is mindfulness, which currently is enjoying great success in psychology: this is the capacity to be conscious of one's experience in the moment, without judging. It is very useful in calming anxiety. It permits us to acknowledge our suffering while understanding that it is temporary. The second component invites us to recognize our common humanity by reminding us of our connection with many other people who have gone through what we're enduring. This prompts us to show kindness to ourselves, as we would to a friend or relative who was going through a rough patch.

When we link unconditional self-acceptance with self-compassion, the two elements consolidate our resilience to stupidity. When we accept ourselves without reservations or conditions, self-compassion becomes easier to put into practice in our daily lives.

The Virtues of the Excuse

Excuses are like an exquisite perfume; they can transform the most awkward moment into a marvelous gift. —Margaret Lee Runbeck

It's well known that an apology can smooth a tense situation when you've done something stupid. When we spill red wine on our host's white carpet, it's a definite blunder that we deeply regret, feeling a range of emotions from embarrassment to guilt. But a quick excuse can make everyone feel more at ease. All actions related to human stupidity can be mitigated by excuses.

However, saying you're sorry isn't always that easy, as the American psychologist Harriet Goldhor Lerner explains.[5] She suggests that making excuses is appropriate when we regret our actions and want to express this in a sincere way to others. In a fairly easygoing way, we can apologize when we've made some gaffe (bumping into someone, making a thoughtless remark, or causing damage, like breaking a glass or dropping a plate). In such cases, excuses alleviate the situation: they allow us not only to feel accepted in an authentic way, but to show others our regret.

But excuses for more serious errors can be trickier to formulate. Sometimes we feel incapable of apologizing, or we fear that the apology itself might put a relationship at risk. However, not apologizing can also be dangerous! In all cases, making an apology puts you on a path that's generally unknown and hard to navigate. But by staying true to our authentic selves, we can find our way.

When Excuses Do Harm

An apology is the superglue of life! It can fix just about anything! –LYNN JOHNSTON

Sometimes our excuses do not hit their targets: perhaps we phrased them badly, or the person we apologized to didn't accept our apology. In the latter case, we have to reboot our self-acceptance and acknowledge that, though this is difficult to admit, our apologies will not always be accepted.

To give our excuses the greatest chance of accomplishing their goal, we should avoid falling into the traps that Harriet Goldhor Lerner lays out.

For instance, if you use a qualifier ("but," "however," etc.), it's easy for an excuse to miss the mark ("I'm sorry I spilled red wine on the carpet, but it's true that a white carpet isn't ideal for a party"). An excuse like that is nothing more, really, than blame cloaked as apology, as in the formulation, "I'm sorry it's so hard for you to deal with the fact that I was clumsy and spilled some wine." That's accusing the other person of having reacted poorly to your stupidity!

We also make our apologies meaningless if, for example, the offended party hesitates to accept them and we express frustration with them. ("I *told* you I was sorry for spilling the wine! What more can I do?") It's true that there's not much we can do in such cases, other than let enough time pass for the individual to recover from his disappointment. Goldhor Lerner explores other inept ways of making apologies, but she underscores the most important fact to retain: a successful apology focuses on the other person. An apology that centers on our own discomfort fails to achieve its end.

Accepting our mistakes allows us not only to get past them but to learn from them: to learn to accept ourselves, to grant ourselves self-compassion during painful moments, to signal our genuineness through sincere and thoughtful apologies to the other person. Who would have imagined there were such advantages to stupidity?

SHAMELESS

Stupidity is also a gift of God, but one mustn't misuse it.

—*Pope John Paul II*

In her work on the power of vulnerability,[1] Brené Brown of the University of Houston tackles the difference between embarrassment, guilt, and shame—typical reactions to our various stupidities. In discussing embarrassment, we've already remarked that it's often short-lived and transitory. Once past, it's transformed into a memory that, more often than not, leads us to laugh at our own stupidity.

Guilt has somewhat more complicated associations, because it implies that a wrong has been done to another party. We don't want to harm others, but our stupidity can have that effect: guilt allows us to recognize that we have caused pain and spurs us not to do it again. Embarrassment and guilt, therefore, are relatively adaptable reactions.

Shame, on the other hand, evokes a difficult experience that can be toxic and hard to overcome, even traumatic. Shame is not only very hard to endure (on an emotional, cognitive, and physiological level), it also can severely damage the ego. It leaves scars and perpetuates itself. Brené Brown has observed that the most adaptable individuals are "resilient" when confronted with shame. This resilience has several elements, the most important of which is to know oneself well enough to prevent shame from arising in certain situations (by identifying one's own personal shame triggers). This lucidity is joined to the capacity for acceptance: in facing our own vulnerability to shame, we are already on the road to accepting our weaknesses and our mistakes. *S. C.*

UNCONDITIONAL SELF-ACCEPTANCE

The idea of unconditional acceptance can clash with our profound beliefs, as we have a tendency to conflate the value of our performance with our worth as human beings. Moreover, unconditional self-acceptance is sometimes confused, wrongly, with self-esteem, which, in its original definition, relied strongly on the notion of performance and proved very unstable over time.[1] Yet, one day or another, in spite of our best efforts, our performance is sure to prove insufficient.

Unconditional self-esteem can be confused with an attitude of resignation, passivity, complacency, pure egotism, or even apathy about our most important goals. Nonetheless, it does not propose that we deny our deficiencies, rather that we simply accept them, learn from them, and resolve to make progress, while maintaining a benevolent attitude of unconditional acceptance of our *being*. S. C.

STUPIDITY IS THE BACKGROUND NOISE OF WISDOM

A Conversation with
> Tobie Nathan <

*Emeritus professor of psychology at the University of Paris
VIII-Vincennes-Saint-Denis, writer, and diplomat*

Q. Does stupidity vary according to culture?

A. Actually, culture serves to preserve stupidity, by generating a large number of complex ideas as a sort of shared philosophy. The more cultivated you are, the more access you have to complex ideas. Even if you are stupid, you are insulated against your own stupidity.

Q. But can you be seen as a fool in one culture and not in another?

A. I'm not sure about that. Stupidity can be recognized, whether in a discussion or in the creation of something: a book, a tool, music. . . . It's through action that intellectual incapacity reveals itself; and the more the action has been culturally organized, the smaller the chance you have of displaying your own stupidity. For example, at universities, most of the philosophers never practice philosophy, they only teach the history of philosophy: "Plato said this, Descartes said that. . . ." They never say, "Me, I say this." If they did, they would reveal their stupidity. The history of philosophy serves to dissimulate their intellectual ineptitude.

Q. **Can fools get ahead by hiding their stupidity behind other people's culture?**

A. They always advance in disguise! The stupider they are, the more they want to prove that they're not; it's a question of pride. So they seek tools elsewhere, everywhere. It's awe-inspiring. Lacan said that when you psychoanalyzed idiots, they turned nasty because they became aware of their inadequacies. That's one of the rare opinions of Lacan that is correct and interesting!

Q. **And what about psychologists? Do they ever utter stupidities?**

A. All the time! I've seen them come and go, the waves of psychology. Back when I was a student, I participated in a study in which five milliliters of ethyl alcohol were injected into our veins. Once we were a little tipsy, we preferred women with big breasts. And voilà, the researchers' hypothesis was proved. I assure you that this was a university study that was published in the *Bulletin de Psychologie*. This is the stupidity that has preoccupied psychologists for fifty years, and that still obsesses them today: the mania for measuring things. Since they had to measure *something*, they measured men's desire for women relative to quantity of alcohol absorbed. No need for a study to show that! I think they're moving a tiny bit beyond that kind of stupidity, but not much. Then again, if they don't measure anything, then what is psychology for? Ah well, it's a problem.... Because then you're forced to have ideas, which is where it gets complicated, because then people can see that you're an idiot. Behind the screen of measurement, it's harder to see. It's a curse for psychology!

Q. Does neuroscience perpetuate this kind of stupidity?

A. They brought a little intelligence and originality into psychology at the beginning, when the most absolute materialism held sway—which was surprising. They should have kept it up, but the scientists didn't have the courage. Neuroscience has decayed and fallen into the same ditch of objectivity. But that's always the way with the sciences: after a great discovery injects ten or twenty years with its dynamism, it peters out in favor of patrons who want to stake their claim: it's finished, there's no more creativity. As for nonstupidity: that's the definition of creativity. And when did we see the last creativity in the subject of psychology? Seventy years ago, maybe.

Q. Overall, would you say we are living in a golden age of stupidity, or that it's just business as usual?

A. When you eliminate the possibility of erudition, and complex big ideas like religion—sacred texts, traditional rites of the people—then stupidity resurfaces. In our era, by renouncing common philosophies, we've forced people to expose their stupidity more visibly. They're not stupider than before, they're possibly even less stupid; but their stupidity is easier to see.

Q. Without erudition and the proper language, stupidity is laid bare?

A. That's exactly right! I couldn't have said it better myself.

Q. So we're both adopting the Socratic method! But what would be the best way to combat stupidity?

A. There isn't one! Why do you want to fight stupidity? You just have to avoid idiots, that's all. Me, I've tried a little, at the university, where idiotic jargon prevails. I'm naïve. It's true! And it shows. . . . I'd thought the university really was intended for research and instruction. So that's what I've engaged with. I've seen the consequences: catastrophe. If you want the slightest chance of continuing to exist in academia, you have to hide. As soon as you show yourself, you become a target. Fools don't like people who aren't fools. I may be one, perhaps, but if they take me for someone who isn't, they won't miss me.

Q. But you write a lot of books, which isn't a very good way of keeping a low profile.

A. That's not at all the same thing as showing up at an administrative council at the university, or a scientific council. Because that's terrifying: a hunting village, but much less developed.

Q. Have you yourself on occasion said or done stupid things that you later regretted?

A. Mistakes, yes. But what are stupidities? To really do something stupid is to persist in error. I've often faced the criticism of my peers. In such cases, one can make honorable amends: "I was mistaken. Psychoanalysis is the most brilliant thing that was ever invented. Mea culpa for what I said." But it's complicated because at the same time you have to save face. Then again, you can persist in error . . . and then you're taken for a fool. Some of my oldest colleagues have tried to mix psychoanalysis and Marxism. If you persist in that today, after you've been shown that psychoanalysis is dead and that Marxism is a disaster in the political arena, then you really can say that you're stupid. Me, I've stuck to my own path, I've continued with ethnopsychiatry. I still don't know if that was a mistake.

Q. What are the worst stupidities that you've been accused of in ethnopsychiatry?

A. It began with my mentor, Georges Devereux. He himself reproached me for my interest in shamanism: "Shamans are all psychotics! They're insane! You don't know them!" Me, I think their techniques are very interesting, as well as the philosophy they convey. I've always thought that we could teach traditional therapies through their techniques. Since these are actual techniques, why not borrow them, adopt them, and apply them ourselves. As long as we understand them. I've been criticized a lot for that. I haven't been told I was stupid, but that I was perverse to defend the backwardness of these people, as if they were a personal cause of mine. Now, nobody attacks me for this anymore. People have understood that those who come from other places don't need us to defend their thinking; they do it very well themselves. We are obliged to live in a world where other cultures don't share our way of thinking. It's hard, but we have to.

Q. **In our age, does stupidity have new playing fields?**

A. I've been one of the most enthusiastic advocates of real, direct democracy. At last, it exists! It's social networks. The people now have a voice as strong as anyone you might name. If you're on Twitter, you have exactly the same level of influence as Emmanuel Macron, even if you have fewer followers. You can speak to him, and he to you. Me, he never talks to me, but in principle it's possible. We hadn't anticipated that in putting this direct democracy into effect, we would reveal the idiocy of three quarters of its users! It's really something to be concerned about.

Q. Do you mean that direct democracy does not show people's intellectual potential?

A. Not at all. It's a real problem. So we have to turn back, educate, instruct, guide people to creativity, make them discover complex thoughts, and give them the desire to wrestle with new ideas. That's what a teacher does, normally. We can't just throw up our hands because of social networks, quite the contrary!

Q. What if people don't want to become intelligent, after all? What if they want to react very quickly and emotionally to things, before moving on to something else?

A. Psychologists often warn us against the laziness of simply giving vent to our emotions. An emotion is compacted intelligence. The smarter you are, the more capable you are of complex emotions. We have to stop putting emotion and intelligence in opposition. Someone who uses his intelligence feels more complex emotions than someone who doesn't. Use your intelligence! I don't mean *you* in particular. It's a catchphrase.

Q. Do you have a chance of being heard?

A. None. It's a shame. In the past, people had a taste for the game of chess, a true intellectual sport, an Olympic category, which attested to the fact that you could use your intelligence like your other muscles. It was a fight to the death: "checkmate" means "the king is dead" in Arabic. Only death contained the complete knowledge of all the game's possibilities. Alas, at the present time, so do computers. If death is not the only key to truth, the game becomes pointless. For a long time, we thought its possibilities were inexhaustible, but now we can't play it anymore! This is a catastrophe bequeathed to us by the twentieth century. In any case, it's not we who are intelligent, it's the tools we make. They force us to think things. We've created a language that forces us to think, and that language is more intelligent than us. There's no abstract intelligence, despite what cognitive scientists say. That's false, it's bullshit! Besides, they themselves are offshoots of the instruments they make. To measure . . . It comes as no shock, it's logical, that at any given moment our tools will become more intelligent than us. The primary thing is that we must remain in competition with them. This is a race we've been running since the dawn of humanity. We're still in it, but I don't know for how much longer. And when I say "we," I don't mean us, the French: but all human beings.

Q. Can we turn stupidity to our advantage? Since all we can do is avoid fools, and we can't change them, should we acknowledge their existence and thank them for something? After all, it's thanks to them that we gain wisdom: the wisdom of keeping a low profile, being patient, indulgent, tolerant. . . .

A. I'm with you, pretty much. I've taught for forty years, to the point that I've been told I was too old (in France, you don't have the right to teach after a certain age, though education is the only place where old people can be useful). At the beginning, you find yourself faced with people who either take you for a guru (which is a catastrophe, a way of burying you alive), or challenge you. When you're young, you're more dynamic but you're impatient, you find it hard to put up with people who don't understand you. You're irritated, furious, you try to convince people, in spite of it all. Over time, it's true that I acquired some patience, and a sort of sympathy for the banality of the world. I tell myself that in music, you have to have a background for the melody to appear. In the same way, stupidity is no more than the background noise that allows us to acquire a little wisdom.

Interview by Jean-François Marmion.

CONTRIBUTORS

DAN ARIELY: James B. Duke Professor of Psychology and Behavioral Economics at Duke University, and the founder of the research institution the Center for Advanced Hindsight. He is the author of *Predictably Irrational: The Hidden Forces That Shape Our Decisions* and *The Honest Truth About Dishonesty: How We Lie to Everyone, Especially Ourselves.*

BRIGITTE AXELRAD: An honorary professor of philosophy and psychosociology. She is the author of *The Ravages of False Memory* and a member of the Zetetic Observatory of Grenoble and of the editorial board of the magazine *Science and Pseudosciences*, a publication edited by the French Association for Scientific Information (AFIS), to which she is a regular contributor.

LAURENT BÈGUE: A senior member of the Institut Universitaire de France, and director of the Maison des Sciences de l'Homme-Alpes. He is the author of *The Psychology of Good and Evil*, *Traité de Psychologie Sociale [A Treatise on Social Psychology]*, and *L'Agression Humaine [Human Aggression]*.

CLAUDIE BERT: A scientific journalist specializing in the social sciences.

STACEY CALLAHAN: A professor of clinical psychology and psychopathology at the University of Toulouse 2-Jean Jaurès, and a researcher at the Centre d'Études et de Recherches en Psychopathologie et Psychologie de la Santé (CERPPS; Center for Studies and Research in Psychopathology and Health Psychology). She is the author of *Les Thérapies Comportmentales et Cognitives: Fondements Théoriques et Applications Cliniques* [*Behavioral and Cognitive Therapies: Theoretical Foundations and Clinical Applications*]; *Cessez de Vous Déprécier! Se Libérer du Syndrome de l'Imposteur* [*Stop Undervaluing Yourself! Shaking the Impostor Complex*], with Kevin Chassangre; and *Mécanismes de Defense et Coping* [*Defense and Coping Mechanisms*], with Henri Chabrol.

JEAN-CLAUDE CARRIÈRE: Screenwriter (*The Return of Martin Guerre, The Controversy of Valladolid, The Circle of Liars, Credo*) for Pierre Étaix, Louis Malle, Luis Buñuel, and Milos Forman, and author, with Guy Bechtel, of *Dictionnaire de la Bêtise et des Erreurs de Jugement* [*Dictionary of Stupidity and Errors in Judgment*].

SERGE CICCOTTI: Doctor of psychology, therapist, and researcher at the University of Bretagne-Sud. He is the author of numerous works of popular psychology, notably *Quand Tu Nages dans le Bonheur, y'a Toujours un Abruti pour Te Sortir de l'Eau* [*When You're Swimming in Happiness, Some Moron Always Plucks You Out of the Water*].

JEAN COTTRAUX: Honorary psychiatrist at the Hôpitaux of the Centre Hospitalier Universitaire (CHU) of Lyon, and former CHU lecturer; founding member of the Academy of Cognitive Therapy of Philadelphia. He is the author of, among other works, *Les Répétitions des Scénarios de Vie* [*Repetitions of Life Patterns*]; *À Chacun Sa Creativité: Einstein, Mozart, Picasso ... et Nous* [*Each to His Own Creativity: Einstein, Mozart, Picasso ... and Us*]; and *Tous Narcissiques* [*We're All Narcissists*].

BORIS CYRULNIK: Neuropsychiatrist and director of education at the University of Toulon. He has published many works, including *Un Merveilleux Malheur* [*Wonderfully Bad Luck*]; *Ivres Paradis, Bonheurs Héroïques* [*Drunken Paradises, Heroic Happinesses*]; and *Les Âmes Blessées* [*Wounded Souls*].

ANTONIO DAMASIO: Professor of neuroscience, neurology, psychology, and philosophy, and director of the Brain and Creativity Institute at the University of Southern California, he is the author of, among other works, *Descartes' Error: Emotion, Reason, and the Human Brain* and *The Strange Order of Things: Life, Feeling, and the Making of Cultures.*

SEBASTIAN DIEGUEZ: Neuropsychologist and researcher at the Laboratory for Cognitive and Neurological Sciences at the Department of Medicine of the University of Fribourg. Author of *Maux d'Artistes: Ce Que Cachent les Oeuvres* [*Artists' Woes: What Works of Art Conceal*] and *Total Bullshit! Aux Sources de la Post-Vérité* [*Total Bullshit! The Roots of Post-Truth*].

JEAN-FRANÇOIS DORTIER: Founder and editorial director of the magazines *Le Cercle Psy* [*Psychological Circle*] and *Sciences Humaines* [*Social Sciences*].

EWA DROZDA-SENKOWSKA: Professor of social psychology at the Université Paris Descartes. She is the editor of the books *Les Pièges du Raisonnement: Comment Nous Nous Trompons en Croyant Avoir Raison* [*Traps of Reasoning: How We Fool Ourselves While Believing We're Right*] and *Menaces Sociales et Environnementales: Repenser la Société des Risques* [*Social and Environmental Threats: Rethinking the Risk Society*].

PASCAL ENGEL: Philosopher and director of studies at L'École des Hautes Études en Sciences Sociales [The School for Advanced Studies in the Social Sciences] in Paris, and author of *La Norme du Vrai* [*The Norm of Truth*]; *Philosophie et Psychologie* [*Philosophy and Psychology*]; *La Dispute* [*The Dispute*]; and *Les Lois de l'Esprit: Julien Benda ou la Raison* [*Laws of the Mind: Julien Benda, or Reason*].

HOWARD GARDNER: The John H. and Elisabeth A. Hobbs Research Professor of Cognition and Education at the Harvard Graduate School of Education. A developmental psychologist, he originated the theory of multiple intelligences. A recipient of the MacArthur Prize (1981), the

Grawemeyer Award in Education (1990), and a Guggenheim Fellowship (2000), he is the author of *Frames of Mind: The Theory of Multiple Intelligences*; *The Unschooled Mind: How Children Think and How Schools Should Teach*; and *Five Minds for the Future*.

NICOLAS GAUVRIT: Psychologist and mathematician, he teaches mathematics at ESPE [*L'École Supérieure du Professorat et de l'Éducation*] Lille Nord de France and is an institutional member of the Human and Artificial Cognition (CHArt) university laboratory. He is the author of *Les Surdoués Ordinaires* [*Ordinary Gifted People*].

ALISON GOPNIK: Professor of psychology and philosophy at the University of California, Berkeley, and author of *The Philosophical Baby: What Children's Minds Tell Us About Truth, Love, and the Meaning of Life*; *The Scientist in the Crib: What Early Learning Tells Us About the Mind* (with Andrew Meltzoff and Patricia Kuhl); and *The Gardener and the Carpenter: What the New Science of Child Development Tells Us About the Relationship Between Parents and Children*.

RYAN HOLIDAY: A former marketing director for American Apparel and columnist for *The New York Observer*, he published three bestsellers on marketing strategy and personal growth before he was twenty-eight: *Growth Hacker Marketing: A Primer on the Future of PR, Marketing, and Advertising*; *The Obstacle Is the Way: The Timeless Art of Turning Trials into Triumph*; and *Trust Me, I'm Lying: Confessions of a Media Manipulator*, in which he explains how easy it was to create buzz for his clients.

AARON JAMES: A philosophy professor at the University of California, Irvine, he is the author of *Assholes: A Theory* and *Assholes: A Theory of Donald Trump*.

FRANÇOIS JOST: Emeritus professor at the Sorbonne Nouvelle-Paris 3 and founder and honorary director of the Centre d'Étude sur les Images et les Sons Médiatique (CEISME; Media Sound and Image Study

Center), he has published more than twenty-five books, including *L'Empire du Loft* [*The Empire of Loft*]; *Le Culte du Banal* [*The Cult of Banality*]; and *La Méchanceté á l'Ère Numérique* [*Bad Luck in the Digital Era*].

DANIEL KAHNEMAN: Emeritus professor of psychology at Princeton University, he won the Nobel Prize in Economics in 2002 for his work on judgment and decision making, conducted largely with his late colleague Amos Tversky. He is also the author of *Thinking, Fast and Slow.*

PIERRE LEMARQUIS: Neurologist and essayist. He is the author of *Sérénade pour un Cerveau Musicien* [*Serenade to a Musician's Brain*]; *L'Empathie Ésthétique: Entre Mozart et Michel-Ange* [*Aesthetic Empathy: Between Mozart and Michelangelo*]; and *Portrait du Cerveau en Artiste* [*Portrait of the Artist's Brain*].

PATRICK MOREAU: Professor of literature at Collège Ahuntsic in Montreal, editor in chief of the magazine *Argument*, and author of *Pourquoi Nos Enfants Sortent-Ils de l'École Ignorants?* [*Why Do Our Children Leave School Knowing Nothing?*] and *Ces Mots Qui Pensent à Notre Place Petits Échantillons de Cette Novlangue Qui Nous Aliène* [*Words That Do Our Thinking for Us: A Sampling of the Newspeak That Alienates Us*].

TOBIE NATHAN: Emeritus professor of psychology at the Université Paris II Vincennes-Saint Denis, he is a leader in the field of ethnopsychiatry, a writer, diplomat, and author of numerous works, including *Ethno-Roman* [*Ethno-Novel*]; *La Folie des Autres* [*The Folly of Others*]; and *Les Âmes Errantes* [*Errant Souls*].

DELPHINE OUDIETTE: Researcher at the Institute of the Brain and the Spinal Cord, with the Motivation, Brain, and Behavior team, she studies the role that sleep and dreams play in major cognitive functions like memory and creativity. She is the author of *Comment Dormons-Nous?* [*How Do We Sleep?*] with Isabelle Arnulf.

EMMANUELLE PIQUET: An exponent of the brief, strategic therapies of the Palo Alto School, she is the first to have developed a mode of intervention to counter school bullying using the theories of the Palo Alto School, and has created centers to implement these interventions, Chagrin Scolaire [Schoolyard Misery] and À 180 Degrés [At 180 Degrees], in France, Switzerland, and Belgium.

PIERRE DE SENARCLENS: Honorary professor of international relations at the Université de Lausanne, he is the author of numerous works on the history of ideas and the history and sociology of international relations. Notable among them are *Mondialisation, Souveraineté, et Théorie des Relations Internationales* [*Globalization, Sovereignty, and International Relations Theory*]; *L'Humanitaire en Catastrophe* [*The Humanitarian in a State of Catastrophe*]; and *Nations et Nationalismes* [*Nations and Nationalisms*].

YVES-ALEXANDRE THALMANN: A doctor of natural sciences, he is a professor of psychology and an instructor at the College Saint-Michel in Fribourg. He is the author of many works, including *Pensée Positive 2.0* [*Positive Thinking 2.0*]; *Apprenez à Conduire Votre Cerveau* [*Learn to Drive Your Brain*]; *On a Toujours une Seconde Chance d'Être Heureux* [*You've Always Got a Second Chance to Be Happy*]; and *Pourquoi les Gens Intelligents Prennent-Ils aussi des Décisions Stupides?* [*Why Do Smart People Make Stupid Choices?*].

NOTES

THE SCIENTIFIC STUDY OF IDIOTS

1. Mara Sidoli, "Farting as a Defence Against Unspeakable Dread," *Journal of Analytical Psychology* 41, no. 2 (April 1996): 165–78.

2. David Graeber, "On the Phenomenon of Bullshit Jobs: A Work Rant," *Strike!* 3, August 2013, www.strikemag.org/bullshit-jobs.

3. Roger C. Schank and Robert P. Abelson, *Scripts, Plans, Goals and Understanding: An Inquiry into Human Knowledge Structures*, chapters 1–3 (Hillsdale, NJ: Lawrence Erlbaum Associates, 1977).

4. Daniel J. Simons and Daniel T. Levin, "Failure to Detect Changes to People During a Real-World Interaction," *Psychonomic Bulletin & Review* 5, no. 4 (1998): 644–49.

5. Ellen J. Langer, "The Illusion of Control," *Journal of Personality and Social Psychology* 32, no. 2 (1975): 311–28.

6. Leo Montada and Melvin J. Lerner, eds., preface to *Responses to Victimizations and Belief in a Just World*, (New York: Springer, 1998) vii-viii.

7. Franck Daninos, "Moto Fantôme de l'A4: Une Harley Peut-Elle Rouler Sans Pilote Sur Plusieurs Kilometres?" [The Phantom Motorcycle of the A4: Can a Harley Travel for Several Kilometers Without a Driver?], Sciencesetavenirs.fr, June 21, 2017.

8. Miron Zuckerman, Jordan Silberman, and Judith A. Hall, "The Relation Between Intelligence and Religiosity: A Meta-Analysis and Some Proposed Explanations," *Personality and Social Psychology Review* 17, no. 4 (August 2013): 325–54.

9. Susan T. Charles, Mara Mather, and Laura L. Carstensen, "Aging and Emotional Memory: The Forgettable Nature of Negative Images for Older Adults," *Journal of Experimental Psychology: General* 132, no. 2 (2003): 310.

10. Georges Brassens, "Le Temps ne Fait Rien à l'Affaire" [Age Has Nothing to Do with It], 1961.

11. Ellen J. Langer, "The Illusion of Control."

12. Shelley E. Taylor and Jonathan D. Brown, "Illusion and Well-Being: A Social Psychological Perspective on Mental Health," *Psychological Bulletin* 103, no. 2 (198), 193–210.

13. Jean-François Verlhiac, "L'Effet de Faux Consensus: Une Revue Empirique et Théorique" [The Effect of False Consensus: An Empirical and Theoretical Review], *L'Année Psychologique* 100 (2000): 141–82.

14. Dale T. Miller and Michael Ross, "Self-Serving Biases in the Attribution of Causality. Fact or Fiction?" *Psychological Bulletin* 82 (1975): 213–25.

15. Justin Kruger and David Dunning, "Unskilled and Unaware of It: How Difficulties in Recognizing One's Own Incompetence Lead to Inflated Self-Assessments," *Journal of Personality and Social Psychology* 77, no. 6 (1999): 1121–34.

16. Steven J. Heine, Shinobu Kitayama, and Darrin R. Lehman, "Cultural Differences in Self-Evaluation: Japanese Readily Accept Negative Self-Relevant Information," *Journal of Cross-Cultural Psychology* 32 (2001): 434–43.

17. Esther R. Greenglass and Juhani Julkunen, "Cynical Distrust Scale," *Personality and Individual Differences* (1989).

18. Paul Rozin and Edward B. Royzman, "Negativity Bias, Negativity Dominance, and Contagion," *Personality and Social Psychology Review* 5 (2001): 296–320.

19. Lee Ross, "The Intuitive Psychologist and His Shortcomings: Distortions in the Attribution Process," *Advances in Experimental Social Psychology* 10 (1977): 173–220.

A TAXONOMY OF MORONS

1. Xavier de La Porte, interview with Gérard Berry, in *L'Obs*, November 21, 2016, www .nouvelobs.com/rue89-le-grand-entretien/20160826.RUE7684/gerard-berry -l-ordinateur-est-completement-con.html.

A THEORY OF ASSHOLES

1. Robert Sutton, professor of management at Stanford University, published *The No Asshole Rule* in 2007, in which he defends the idea of a professional environment free of assholes, particularly sexual harassers.

FROM STUPIDITY TO HOGWASH

1. Robert Musil, *Über die Dummheit*, 1937.

2. Kevin Mulligan, *Anatomie della Stoltezza* [*Anatomies of Foolishness*] (Milano: Jouvence, 1996).

3. Harry G. Frankfurt, *On Bullshit* (Princeton, NJ: Princeton University Press, 1992).

4. Georges Picard, *De la Connerie* [*On Stupidity*] (Paris: Éditions Corti, 1994).

5. Alain Roger, *Bréviaire de la Bêtise* [*A Breviary of Stupidity*] (Paris: Gallimard, 2008).

TO BE HUMAN IS TO BE EASILY FOOLED

1. Rolf Dobelli, *The Art of Thinking Clearly* (New York: HarperCollins, 2013).

2. Kathryn Schulz, *Being Wrong: Adventures in the Margin of Error* (New York: Harper-Collins, 2010).

3. Daniel Kahneman, *Thinking Fast and Slow* (New York: Farrar, Straus & Giroux, 2011).

LET JUSTICE DO ITS WORK (OF DIGESTION)

1. Shai Danziger, Jonathan Levav, and Liora Avnaim-Pesso, "Extraneous Factors in Judicial Decisions," *Proceedings of the National Academy of Sciences* 108, no. 17 (April 26, 2011).

CRITIQUE OF THE PURE REASONER

1. Jean-François Bonnefon, *Le Raisonneur et Ses Modèles* [*The Reasoner and His Models*] (Grenoble, France: PUG, 2011).

ON STUPIDITY IN THE BRAIN

1. A recent article of high caliber was voluntarily suppressed by members of the neurological community, particularly those affiliated with university hospitals. The article reports that taking early retirement increases the risk of contracting Alzheimer's by 15 percent. Out of solidarity, I will not give my sources, for fear that they might be misused and wrongly interpreted by the French government's health ministry.

INTENTIONAL IDIOCY

1. Robert J. Sternberg, ed., *Why Smart People Can Be So Stupid* (New Haven, CT: Yale University Press, 2003).
2. Keith E. Stanovich, *What Intelligence Tests Miss: The Psychology of Rational Thought* (New Haven, CT: Yale University Press, 2009).
3. Sophie Brasseur and Catherine Cuche, *Le Haut Potentiel en Questions* [*High Potential in Questions*] (Wavre, Belgium: Mardaga, 2017).
4. Keith E. Stanovich, Richard F. West, and Maggie E. Toplak, *The Rationality Quotient: Toward a Test of Rational Thinking* (Cambridge, MA: MIT Press, 2016).

WHEN VERY SMART PEOPLE BELIEVE VERY DUMB THINGS

1. Gérald Bronner, *La Démocratie des Crédules* [*The Democracy of the Gullible*] (Paris: Presse Universitaires de France, 2013), 296.
2. Miron Zuckerman, Jordan Silberman, and Judith A. Hall, "The Relation Between Intelligence and Religiosity: A Meta-Analysis and Some Proposed Explanations," *Personality and Social Psychology Review* 17, no. 4 (August 2013): 325–54.
3. Heather A. Butler, "Who Do Smart People Do Foolish Things? Intelligence Is Not the Same as Critical Thinking and the Difference Matters," *Scientific American*, October 3, 2017.
4. *Les Lois de l'Attraction Mentale* [*The Laws of Mental Attraction*], directed by Loki Jackal (Nancy, France: La Tronche en Biais, November 2017), documentary.
5. John Stachel, David C. Cassidy, Robert Schulmann, eds., *Collected Papers of Albert Einstein, The Early Years 1899–1902* (Princeton, NJ: Princeton University Press, 1987).

WHY WE FIND MEANING IN COINCIDENCES

1. Nicolas Gaufrit, *Vous Avez Dit Hasard?: Entre Mathématiques et Psychologie* [*Did You Say Luck?: Between Mathematics and Psychology*] (Paris: Humensis, 2014).

2. *Editor's Note:* A theory elaborated by Anne Ancelin Schützenberger, inspired by psychoanalysis, psychotherapy, and psychodynamics, which proposes that tensions and traumatizing events endured by one's ancestors can condition the psychological problems and behaviors of a subject.

3. *Editor's Note:* A meaningful coincidence for the observer, produced by "significant and creatively productive chance," according to Carl Gustav Jung.

THE LANGUAGE OF STUPIDITY

1. Picard, *De la Connerie.*

2. George Orwell, *1984* (London: Secker and Warburg, 1949).

3. Éric Chauvier, *Les Mots Sans les Choses* [*Words Without Things*] (Paris: Editions Allia, 2014), 76.

4. It is this "indifference to reality" that is, according to Harry G. Frankfurt, "the very essence of stupidity." Cf. Harry G. Frankfurt, *On Bullshit* (Princeton, NJ: Princeton University Press, 1992), 34.

5. Claude Hagège, *L'Homme de Paroles,* [*The Man of Words*] (Paris: Fayard, 1985), 202.

6. Cf. Jacques Dewitte, "La Lignification de la Langue" [The Lignification of Language], *Hermès, La Revue,* no. 58 (March 2010): 48–49.

7. René Zazzo, who calls the inability of the subject to "decenter" himself and "to see through other's eyes" one of the principal sources of stupidity. Cf. "Qu'est-ce que la Connerie, Madame?" [What Is Stupidity, Madame?] in *Où en Est la Psychologie de l'Enfant?* [*Where Are We in Child Psychology?*] by René Zazzo (Paris: Denoël, 1983), 52.

8. Statements marked by stupidity and empty words chiefly reflect herd instincts. Theodor Adorno writes that they "seem to guarantee, even as they leave your mouth, that you're not doing what you're doing," which is bleating "with the crowd." Cf. Theodor Adorno, *The Jargon of Authenticity* (New York: Routledge Classics, 2003), 60.

STUPIDITY AND NARCISSISM

1. René Zazzo, *Où en Est la Psychologie de l'Enfant?* [*Where Are We in Child Psychology?*] (Paris: Denoël, 1984).

2. *Diagnostic and Statistical Manual of Mental Disorders* (*DSM-5*) (Issy les Moulineaux, France: Elsevier Masson, 2015).

3. Jerald Kay, "Toward a Clinically More Useful Model for Diagnosing Narcissistic Personality Disorder," *American Journal of Psychiatry* 165, no. 11 (2007): 1379–382.

4. Frederick S. Stinson, Deborah A. Dawson, Rise B. Goldstein, S. Patricia Chou, Boji Huang, Sharon M. Smith, W. June Ruan, Attila J. Pulay, Tulshi D. Saha, Roger P. Pickering, and Bridget F. Grant, "Prevalence, Correlates, Disability, and Comorbidity of DSM-IV Narcissistic Personality Disorder: Results from the Wave 2 National Epidemiologic Survey on Alcohol and Related Conditions," *Journal of Clinical Psychiatry* 69 (2008): 1033–45.

5. Jean M. Twenge and W. Keith Campbell, *The Narcissism Epidemic* (New York: Atria, 2009).

6. Eric Russ, Jonathan Shedler, Rebekah Bradley, and Drew Westen, "Refining the Construct of Narcissistic Personality Disorder: Diagnostic Criteria and Subtypes," *American Journal of Psychiatry* 165, no. 11 (2008): 1473–81.

7. Christopher Lasch, *The Culture of Narcissism* (New York: W. W. Norton, 1979).

8. Daniel N. Jones and Delroy L. Paulhus, "Introducing the Short Dark Triad (SD30): A Brief Measure of Dark Personality Traits," *Assessment* 21, no. 1 (2014): 28–41.

9. Ernest H. O'Boyle, Donelson R. Forsyth, George. C. Banks, and Michael A. McDaniel, "A Meta-Analysis of the Dark Triad and Work Behavior: A Social Exchange Perspective," *Journal of Applied Psychology* 97, no. 30 (2012): 557–79.

10. Robert Sutton, excerpt from "Are You a Certified Asshole," *The No Asshole Rule* (New York and Boston: Business Plus, 2007).

11. Christopher J. Carpenter, "Narcissism on Facebook: Self-Promotional and Anti-Social Behavior," *Personality and Individual Differences* 52 (2012): 482–86.

12. J. A. Lee and Yongjun Sung, "Hide-and-Seek: Narcissism and 'Selfie'-Related Behavior," *Cyberpsychology, Behavior and Social Networking* 19, no. 5 (May 2016): 347–51.

13. Silvia Casale, Giulia Fioravanti, and Laura Rugai, "Grandiose and Vulnerable Narcissists: Who Is at Higher Risk for Social Networking Addiction?" *Cyberpsychology, Behavior and Social Networking* 19, no. 8 (2016): 510–15.

14. Maeve Duggan, "Online Harassment," Pew Research Center, October 22, 2014, www.pewinternet.org/2014/10/22/online-harassment.

15. Erin E. Buckle, Paul D. Trapnell, and Delroy L. Paulhus, "Trolls Just Want to Have Fun," *Personality and Individual Differences* 67 (2014): 97–102.

STUPID AND EVIL SOCIAL NETWORKS

1. François Jost, *La Méchanceté en Actes à l'Ere Numérique* [*Evil Deeds in the Digital Age*] (Paris: CNRS Éditions, 2018).

2. Web 2.0 refers to the second stage of development of the World Wide Web (now known retrospectively as Web 1.0), featuring increased interactivity, collaboration, and communication channels, and the extensive presence of user-generated content.

3. Guy Debord, *La Société du Spectacle* [*The Society of the Spectacle*] (Paris: Folio 1996).

4. Thomas Coëffé, "Étude: Les Images sur Twitter Permettent de Booster l'Engagement," [Images on Twitter Can Boost Engagement] BDM Media Blog, October 7, 2013, www.blogdumoderateur.com/twitter-images-engagement.

5. "Le Philosophe Masqué," [The Masked Philosopher], interview with Christian Delacampagne, February 1980, in *Le Monde*, April 6, 1980, reprinted in *Dits et Écrits*, vol. IV (Paris: Gallimard Quarto, 2001), text no. 285.

6. *Défi du Sauté dans l'Eau La Chute du Rire* [*The Water Plunge Challenge: The Torrent of Laughter*], YouTube, June 9, 2014, www.youtube.com/watch?v=TwIuTLBmEkE, accessed March 24, 2018.

7. I have preserved the spelling used in the comments.

8. *Un Dîner (Presque) Parfait [An (Almost) Perfect Dinner]*, www.youtube.com/watch?v= M&trhwLQ3QQ.

ANIMATED WISDOM

1. Vladimir Jankélévitch, *L'Innocence et la Méchanceté [Innocence and Evil]* (Paris: Flammarion, coll. Champs, 1986).

2. Adèle Van Reeth and Michaël Foessel, *La Méchanceté [Evil]* (Paris: Plon-France, 2014), 95.

3. Harry G. Frankfurt, *On Bullshit* (Princeton, NJ: Princeton University Press, 1992), 32.

THE INTERNET: THE DEATH OF INTELLIGENCE?

1. Howard Gardner, *Truth, Beauty and Goodness Reframed* (New York: Basic Books, 2011).

2. There's no accounting for taste.

STUPIDITY AND POST-TRUTH

1. Armand Farrachi, *Le Triomphe de la Bêtise [The Triumph of Stupidity]* (Arles, France: Actes Sud, 2018).

2. Sebastian Dieguez, *Total Bullshit! Au Coeur de la Post-Vérité [Total Bullshit! At the Heart of Post-Truth]* (Paris: Presse Universitaires de France, 2018).

3. Harry G. Frankfurt, *On Bullshit* (Princeton, NJ: Princeton University Press, 1992).

4. "Word of the Year, 2016," en.oxforddictionaries.com/word-of-the-year/word-of-the-year-2016.

5. Pascal Engel, "The Epistemology of Stupidity," in *Performance Epistemology: Foundations and Applications*, ed. M. A. Fernández Vargas (Oxford: Oxford University Press, 2016): 196–223.

6. Alain Roger, *Bréviaire de la Bêtise [A Bréviary of Stupidity]* (Paris: Gallimard, 2008); see also Michel Adam, *Essai sur la Bêtise [Essays on Stupidity]* (Paris: La Table Ronde, 2004).

7. Laura Penny, *Your Call Is Important to Us: The Truth About Bullshit* (New York: Three Rivers Press, 2005).

8. Belinda Cannone, *La Bêtise S'Améliore* (Paris: Pocket, 2016).

9. Raymond Nickerson, "Confirmation Bias: A Ubiquitous Phenomenon in Many Guises," *Review of General Psychology* 2 (1998): 175–220.

10. Oliver Hahl, Minjae Kim, and Ezra W. Z. Sivan, "The Authentic Appeal of the Lying Demagogue: Proclaiming the Deeper Truth About Political Illegitimacy," *American Sociological Review* 83 (2018): 1–33.

11. Keith E. Stanovich, "Rationality, Intelligence and Levels of Analysis in Cognitive Science: Is Dysrationalia Possible?" in *Why Smart People Can Be So Stupid*, ed. R. Sternberg (New Haven, CT: Yale University Press, 2002): 124–58.

12. Barbara K. Hofer and Paul R. Pintrich, eds., *Personal Epistemology: The Psychology of Beliefs About Knowledge and Knowing* (Mahwah, NJ: Lawrence Erlbaum Associates, 2002).

13. Let us note that it is also very difficult for a rational, intelligent person to imagine the mental world of a fool, a phenomenon sometimes called "the curse of knowledge." Susan A. J. Birch and Paul Bloom, "The Curse of Knowledge in Reasoning About False Beliefs," *Psychological Science* 18 (2007): 382–86.

14. David Dunning, "The Dunning-Kruger Effect: On Being Ignorant of One's Own Ignorance," *Advances in Experimental Social Psychology* 44 (2011): 247–96.

15. "Brandolini's Law," *Ordres Spontane Blog*, August 7, 2014, ordrespontane.blogspot.ch /2014/07/brandolinis-law.html.

16. Sebastian Dieguez, "Qu'est-ce Que La Bêtise?" [What Is Stupidity?], *Cerveau & Psycho* 70 (2015): 84–90.

17. Stefaan Blancke, Maarten Boudry, and Massimo Pigliucci, "Why Do Irrational Beliefs Mimic Science? The Cultural Evolution of Pseudoscience," *Theoria* 83 (2017): 78–98.

18. Adrian Piper, "Pseudorationality," in *Perspectives on Self-Deception*, eds., B. McLaughlin and A. Rorty (Oakland: University of California Press, 1988), 173–97.

19. Robert Musil, *De la Bêtise* [*On Stupidity*] (Paris: Editions Allia, 1937).

20. Justin Tosi and Brandon Warmke, "Moral Grandstanding," *Philosophy and Public Affairs* 44 (2016): 197–217; M. J. Crockett, "Moral Outrage in the Digital Age," *Nature Human Behaviour* 1 (2017): 769–71.

THE METAMORPHOSES OF NATIONALIST FOLLY

1. Ernst Cassirer, *The Myth of the State* (New Haven: CT: Yale University Press, 1966), 3.

2. Jean-Pierre Vernant, *Mythe & Société en Grèce Ancienne* [*Myth and Society in Ancient Greece*] (Paris: La Découverte, 1974), 201.

3. Pierre de Senarclens, "Nations et Nationalisme," *Sciences Humaines*, 2018.

4. Georges Devereux, "La Psychanalyse Appliquée a l'Histoire de Sparte" [Psychoanalysis Applied to the History of Sparta], in *Annales. Histoire, Sciences Sociales* [*Annals. History, Social Sciences*], 20th Century Year, no. 1 (January–February 1965): 31–32.

5. François Hourmant, *Le Désenchantement des Clercs* [*The Disenchantment of the Bureaucrats*] (Rennes, France: Presse Universitaire du Rennes, 1997); Thierry Wolton, *Histoire Mondiale du Communisme* [*The Global History of Communism*], vol. 3: *Les Complices* [*The Accomplices*] (Paris: Grasset, 2017).

HOW CAN WE FIGHT COLLECTIVE ERROR?

1. Christian Morel, *Les Décisions Absurdes* [*Absurd Decisions*] (Paris: Gallimard, 2002), 202; *Les Décisions Absurdes II: Comment Les Éviter* [*Absurd Decisions II: How to Avoid Them*] (Paris: Gallimard, 2012); and *Les Décisions Absurdes III: L'Enfer des Règles, les Pièges Relationnels* [*Absurd Decisions III: The Hell of Rules, and Relational Traps*] (Paris: Gallimard, 2018).

THE HUMAN: THE ANIMAL THAT DARES ALL

1. Audrey Jougla, *Profession: Animal de Laboratoire* [*Job: Lab Animal*] (Paris: Autrement, 2015).

2. Thomas Lepeltier, *L'Imposture Intellectuelle des Carnivores* [*The Intellectual Imposture of Carnivores*] (Paris: Max Milo Éditions, 2017).

3. A.-J. Bouglione, *Contre L'Exploitation Animale* [*Against Animal Exploitation*] (Paris: Tchou, 2018).

4. Marc Bekoff, *Les Émotions des Animaux* [*The Emotions of Animals*] (Paris: Payot, 2009).

5. Yves Christen, *L'Animal Est-Il Une Personne?* [*Are Animals People?*] (Paris: Flammarion, 2009).

6. Florence Burgat, *L'Animal dans les Pratiques de Consommation* [*Animals and the Habits of Consumption*] (Paris: Presse Universitaires de France, 1998).

7. Martin Gibert, *Voir Son Steak Comme un Animal Mort* [*Seeing Your Steak as a Dead Animal*] (Montreal: Lux Éditeur, 2015).

8. Renan Larue, *Le Végétarisme et Ses Ennemis: Vingt-Cinq Siècles de Débats* [*Vegetarianism and Its Foes: Twenty-Five Centuries of Debate*] (Paris: Presse Universitaires de France, 2015).

WHAT CAN BE DONE ABOUT ASSHOLES?

1. In the context of this article, the word "asshole," used generically, enfolds the female counterpart.

2. The inclination to mock his subject will lead him again and again to disavow his role, saying, "He's just being a wimp," or "Quit playing the victim," or in a still more cunning spin, "Victimization is a serious charge."

MAKING PEACE WITH YOUR STUPIDITY

1. Albert Ellis, *Reason and Emotion in Psychotherapy* (New York: Citadel, 1994).

2. Albert Ellis and Robert A. Harper, *A Guide to Rational Living* (Chatsworth, CA: Wilshire Book Company, 1975).

3. Christopher K. Germer, *L'Autocompassion* [*Self-Compassion*] (Paris: Odile Jacob, 2013).

4. Kristin Neff, *Loving Yourself* (New York: HarperCollins, 2011).

5. Harriet G. Lerner, *Why Won't You Apologize?: Healing Betrayals and Everyday Hurts* (New York: Touchstone, 2017).

SHAMELESS

1. Brené Brown, *Daring Greatly: How the Courage to Be Vulnerable Transforms the Way We Live, Love, Parent, and Lead* (New York: Avery), 2012.

UNCONDITIONAL SELF-ACCEPTANCE

1. H. Chabrol, A. Rousseau, and S. Callahan, "Preliminary Results of a Scale Assessing Instability of Self-Esteem," *Canadian Journal of Behavioural Science/Revue Canadienne des Sciences du Comportement* 38, no. 2 (2006): 136–41.